BUDDHA AND BUDDHISM

Maurice Percheron

Translated from the French by
Edmund Stapelton

THE OVERLOOK PRESS
Woodstock, New York

Overlook edition first published in 1982 by

The Overlook Press
Lewis Hollow Road
Woodstock, New York 12498

Copyright © 1956 Editions du Seuil
First published in France by Editions du Seuil, Paris
Translated from the French Le Bouddha et Le Bouddhisme
Translation copyright © Longmans, Green & Co. Ltd. 1957

Library of Congress Cataloging in Publication Data
Percheron, Maurice, 1891-
Buddha and Buddhism.

(Overlook spiritual masters series ; 2)
Translation of: Le Bouddha et le bouddhisme.
Reprint. Originally published: New York :
Harper, 1957 (Men of wisdom ; 3)
1. Buddhism. I. Title. II. Series.
BQ266.P4713 1982   294.3   82-3471
ISBN 0-87951-157-5   AACR2

Printed in the U.S.A.

CONTENTS

PRE-BUDDHIST INDIA

It is impossible to imagine a spiritual movement isolated in time and in space. Every fresh attempt made by man to get nearer the core of the questions which concern his own essence, origin and development is a point in a sequence and, what is more, the culmination of millions of thoughts which went before. Often it is a reaction against them: sometimes even a return to original concepts from which they have deviated: these then tend to be brought back to light by the reform, although seemingly forgotten by consciousness and lodged by now only in the deepest strata of the psyche.

Although we are apt to think of Buddhism as an historical event, the phenomenal aspect of things is entirely alien to it. It has never exhibited a fortuitous or unexpected character; it *had* to happen, and if it had not been formulated in the fifth century before our era, would inevitably have appeared in the following decades, whether they amounted to fifty or a hundred.

This means that we cannot speak of the Buddha or of primitive Buddhism without plotting the position of India, socially and metaphysically, at this period. The Master's message cannot be accurately described as heresy: the latter normally presents an aggressive character of discontinuity which has never been evident in the Doctrine. Rather might one say that the religious sclerosis in which India was embalmed had for almost a millennium concealed a germ that was slowly taking shape.

At its inception, to be sure, Buddhism had no very exhausting battles to fight. In the first place, because it was not stamped with a sufficiently obvious revolutionary character to arouse a vigorous reaction from the Indian conceptions which it was going to prune, by degrees, to their very roots. Secondly, because it was formed in a region where the Brahmins as yet exercised no great power: epigraphy and archaeology prove in fact that in the fifth century before our era Bihār and Nepal had

Brahmā

5

not been deeply penetrated by Indo-European influence. Lastly, the kings and warriors who constituted the Kshatriya caste were secretly struggling to prevent the Brahmins divesting them of their power: they accordingly supported a Buddhism which sapped the strength of the rival theocratic caste by laicizing Brahmanism.

It is not heresy we find in Buddhism, nor even some extension or restatement of Brahmanism, but a parallel development of doctrines with strong reciprocal influence. When in the second century of our era the doctrine of Buddhism is codified many echoes of the old Brahmanism are to be heard in it. In the same way the Hinduism of the sixth century A.D. represents a 'Buddhistic' Brahmanism.

This is why it has been said that the Buddha was not an innovator. Indeed King Aśoka had the Master's teachings carved on stone but omitted to mention his name. Anticipating Nietzsche, this monarch saw a philosopher simply as one who becomes aware of the unformulated thoughts of his time and puts them into spoken or written form; other men then become aware of these thoughts, which they were previously unable to express.

For the humble believer as for the philosopher there was however, from the sixth century B.C., something still more important than the echoes of the Brahmanist pantheon: I refer to the awakening of interest in the soul.

Mankind in India had at first thought of the underworld and the abode of the gods as a last haven where mortal souls received their reward or punishment. Completely foreign to such religion was any idea that death held wanderings, alternations of life and death, for the soul: each man, after leaving the earth, remained fixed for ever, according to his deeds, in the abode of the blessed or in the anguish of a kingdom of darkness.

But later it was supposed that the soul was eternal, only leaving one bodily form to enter another, which might be higher or lower in the scale according to the virtues and sins of its previous incarnation. As a matter of fact, this belief in transmigration already existed here and there in the dim era when the Vedas (Books of Knowledge) were compiled.

At that time *karman*, a subtle substance attached for the time being to a body, represented the acts and their consequences: it was the bond between one existence and the next, the persistence of an irreducible element—in modern terms, a psychic nucleus.

ĀTMAN—BRAHMAN

Ātman: After the end of the Vedic period, as it is called, Brahmanism is characterized by the polarity of ĀTMAN and BRAHMAN.

The ĀTMAN (fancifully explained as 'This me': *At+man*), eleventh of the vital breaths, is that which subsists in the individual beyond any existence, which is associated with the spirit (the principle of life and cognition), and which constitutes the spiritual stuff not only of man but of all things. Ātman represents unity posited behind an apparent diversity and duality. Always present, it functions in the outer world as agent of all perception; yet in its own domain it is not concerned with seeing or hearing: where the absolute reigns, 'all distinction between hearer and heard, seer and seen, disappears'.

With the cessation of consciousness that accompanies the death of an individual, duality, inner and outer, disappears. Now as soon as there is no longer duality, one can no longer see, hear or feel what is Other, and all perception of object or being vanishes. Whereas there is infinite scope for plurality in the boundless multiplicity of the outer world, all this ceases in the womb of absolute Being.

Brahman: BRAHMAN (see Glossary) meant at first the primordial Force which man discerns in every unusual or inexplicable phenomenon (*Mana*). Since the manifestation of this Force was brought about by means of sacrifice—the aim of which was to direct its activity to the advantage of the individual—and this sacrifice depended on the proper recitation of formulae, Brahman

7

was identified with holy prayer, with speech, with the Word. Later on, it became the very principle of the universe.

A new sphere of ideas had thus come to the fore, and the sacred spoken word destined to unite the sacrificer's Ātman with Brahman asserted itself as a cosmic force. A perpetual correspondence was being established between the universe and the essential self of each living being. The monotheism, whose many facets had been reflected in the various divinities, was now made explicit by the irruption of a universal god on to the mental scene. This, however, was not the Great Judge before whom each must give account of his existence—for it was no other than the worshipper's own Self. The confusion of these concepts dissolved happily into concord, in the universality of breath and force wherever they may be, and their fusion in the universe, through their actual identity.

A transition period between the age of the great Vedic gods and Brahmanism proper was probably provided by asceticism. Yogins had for thousands of years been meditating, and training their one or two disciples to spread an unorthodox teaching. Proof of this we have in the Buddha's own search for truth, which he hoped to discover from just such ascetics. The belief was firmly established that asceticism helped towards an understanding of salvation, and conferred miraculous powers through sheer intensity of mortification. The ascetic was thus in a position to vie with the mighty in this world or the other, had a vision of the ultimate aim of life, and slaked his burning thirst for holiness. Less nobly, sometimes, he would hope to gain sufficient power to avenge some indignity.

The association of theories about the universe and God with sacrifice was finally broken by the *Upanishads* ('Confidential lectures'), stemming from the technical discussions, by Brahmins, of Brahman known as *brahmodyas*, the earliest of which probably go back to the first millennium. The *Upanishads* protested for all that against the discontinuance of sacrifice in their religion, and this ground they had in common with the *Āran-*

yakas or 'Forest Treatises'. By now it was time for the notion of personal salvation to be outlined and to become a new, higher experience. Something entirely new, the linking of the Ātman with transmigration, then became solidly established, with the aid of the new term KARMAN.

KARMAN

The idea had found expression that all was not ended after death, and that the impalpable force which dwells in a living body would return to an earthly existence. The exponents of this view, ascetics and men of religion, corresponded to an image-force from the realm of the unconscious, viz. the desire for some form of persistence. To it, of course, they joined such sanctions as a good or wicked life might demand.

Thus unfolded the idea of transmigration—probably one that had long had its place somewhere in the Indian mind—translating, in reality, the hoard of a collective inheritance present in every individual. For the benefit of the crowd, the soul was individualized; the theory revealed it living through a host of existences of a quality dependent on its deserts, and able to go on, from man, to plant, animal, or temporary deity. The bond uniting one life with the next was named KARMAN.

The word is self-explanatory: by derivation *karman* in Sanskrit means 'action', hence by extension a succession of actions. Now what is an action but the manifestation of an inner substance which governs it? So karman unites the sense of work, activity, with that of a subtle matter implanted in the body. It goes from existence to existence clothing itself in new bodily forms in accordance with the consequences of thoughts, words and deeds, with certain propensities of its own, and also with terms of reincarnation. We used above the expression 'irreducible nucleus of psychic energy', which seems the closest approximation to the Indian concept. To this we must add, 'exposed to various contingencies during its wanderings'.

In this way karman took on a distinctly individual character, and corresponded with the powerful universal mechanism which, in later existences, satisfied an appetite never appeased here on earth: the longing for an equitable distribution of destinies, for the rewarding of merit and the punishment of shortcomings. This desire may well have been latent since the beginnings of human consciousness, but scarcely appeared with such clarity until around the third millennium.

Very soon transmigration was not enough for the Hindu. It dawned upon him that works alone cannot bring Beatitude. He wanted more than the knowledge that his subtle essence was immortal yet vagrant. Might one not hope never to be reborn again, even under the best conditions? People yearned to be freed from any sort of 'works' and from all the fruits of action. The eternal Ātman ought to be able to rise above rewards and penalties.

In that case, deliverance lay in Ātman-Brahman. 'He who grasps the Ātman becomes insensitive to pleasure and pain, indifferent to everything; he overcomes the afflictions of the heart. For him there no longer exist father or mother, gods or vedas, life or death. He is in a position to utter the Master-word TAT TVAM ASI (Thou art That).' In other words, 'You—your true being, your spirit—are One with Oneness in the All. Therefore, you are in this All; you are the All.'

Thus Ātman, i.e. Self in man and Self in the universe, is bound, fused, identified in fact, with Brahman: as soon as a being sees that it and the Infinite are but one, it attains to felicity; it is liberated from its migratory nature and from the everlasting rebirths.

There was one problem that had to be solved: how to grasp the Ātman. Use was naturally made of the old practices, but this time with a precise sense of direction given them. Sacrifices, marks of piety such as the butter-offering for the holy lamps, and good conduct constituted the first steps towards spiritual liberation. The yogins supplied ascetic methods of self-mastery and of meditation.

But this was plainly not enough, and only led after all to saintliness: effort or virtuosity by themselves have never given anyone Understanding. It is beyond any scholarship, reasoning, analysis, ecstasy or contemplation on the part of the unaided individual. He learns that he needs a guide: 'In order to attain Understanding one must be instructed by a spiritual adviser.'

It might have been feared that the holy man would seize this opportunity of asserting his power. But the Ātman-Brahman theory proved strong enough to transcend profane considerations. The counsellor remained strictly limited to such training as would lead the person concerned to mystical experience. 'No one else can describe. I alone can assay.' No one could communicate his own experience, not even a guide who had *really* crossed the threshold. The possibility of gaining ultimate revelation was reserved to the person taught, whose business alone it was. The idea of a kind of Grace had taken root: but a Grace which was induced and conditioned.

It is in the Vedānta that we find the universal whole which Brahman represents, and the illusory nature of the diversity and plurality with which man is beset until he has attained entire Understanding, given their most profound expression. By the time of the Buddha, the Atman-Brahman idea had taken firm root and was accepted as fact. No room was left for feeling, or for respite for the soul—which can only thrive when it dissolves in the heart of the universe.

If the gods were still honoured, solicited and feared, they were no longer equal to the problem, which became ever more pressing, of 'Why do we live?' The resemblance of their existence to that of human beings and the instability of their exalted state could not fail, eventually, to weaken their prestige on earth. Particularly since their representatives—hence, they themselves —did not always answer one's questions.

Indian uneasiness had been offered a certain theory of deliverance, credit for which is due not so much to the Brahmins who adopted it for their own benefit, as to the Kshatriyas and, above all, the yogins.

The 'Sankhya' doctrine (Skt. *Sāṃkhya*, 'enumeration') was practised by ascetics, who sought to explain the world with the aid of a thorough-going system of speculation. So far from being an illusion, the world was traced back to two substantial first principles: the lower principle (*Prakṛti*, matter) and the spiritual one (*Purusha*). They envisaged no unity, no Brahman underlying this diversity; and excluded Ātman as well. But they evinced a belief in metempsychosis, along with the idea of a multitude of eternal souls chained up in the bonds of matter.

This obviously very atheistical doctrine, rationalist as it was, and so deeply imbued with a sense of the reality of world and matter, was of course bound to conduce to a strict asceticism. Much later on, the idea that individual souls are independent was to make it possible to build Sivaism on the concept of a sentient immortality.

The point to bear in mind about the Sāmkhya doctrine is that nearly all the ascetics were Kshatriyas. It was in fact customary for a noble, after properly fulfilling his caste-obligations, to renounce secular life when middle-aged and retire far from the world: there to immerse himself in meditation and try to release himself from the succession of rebirths. The Upanishads moreover give us clear evidence of a freethinking in religious matters which is Kshatriya in origin. When the Brahmins took over the idea of deliverance, they owned that 'it is contrary to the natural order that a Brahmin receive instruction from a warrior'.

The religious theory of India, originating in Indo-Iranian and perhaps also Mesopotamian circles, had shifted its centre of gravity, therefore, from outer to inner concerns. The alliance of

A Yogi in India.

man with deity to their mutual defence and protection had been replaced by personal preoccupation with the future of one's soul. Power and well-being, the possession of goods and the fear of ill-defined forces had given way to an intentness on everlasting peace. What now were earthly or supernatural foes, compared with those real antagonists which dwell within a man's soul, and must be fought and overcome? There was evidently no need of Brahmins, since each person had only himself to reckon with, to assure his own soul of bliss.

This transition was not without its weaknesses, however, and called for a Reformation. Yet the Indian mind did not feel strong enough to proceed any farther. Involved as their cogitations on the essence and evolution of the individual soul were, no one defined anything, demonstrated anything, even really investigated anything, or showed any bewilderment at the absurdity of the contradictions.

If as is likely there were, before the Buddha, sages who had a new metaphysical and philosophic view, their word had to contend with firmly rooted popular beliefs, customs and moral principles. A hero was needed to challenge the *status quo*—one resolved to enforce heterodoxy by the strength of his personality.

Buddhism was no more at first than a very limited movement affecting only individuals of heterodox persuasion, whom it conquered one by one; it only took on the aspect of a true reform when the Buddha was represented after his death as a divine emanation, incarnate in a Personage of unique prowess. Legend seized hold of his earthly life, linked it with existing gods (also altering the paradisean arrangements to suit the needs of the case), and filled it with astonishing occurrences of a miraculous nature. This price had to be paid before the Master's word could have any effect on the masses.

The philosophical conception summed up in the words 'The realm of ultimate bliss is within your grasp', the people were in the end to turn into a religion—not in the original sense as derived from Lat. *religare* (to *bind* the adepts), but in that of an otherworldly adoration, complete with rites and propitiatory cult.

THE LEGENDARY LIFE OF THE BUDDHA

The use which the scriptures of Buddhism make, at every turn, of episodes from the Buddha's life, and the minute attention with which iconography refers to them, make it quite impossible to disregard legend and to get at the heart of the Doctrine without being acquainted with the outstanding events of the Sage's earthly existence. They abound, in any case, with a symbolism which lends support or interpretation to the Law. Yet the life of the Buddha in itself has less importance in the practice of Buddhism than might be supposed: the historical Sākyamuni, immune from the ordinary workings of fate as he appears, fades before the archetypal Buddha.

At every turn we glimpse features of the Buddha in the legend which it could not have invented out of nothing. The very fact that the new spiritual laws said to have been brought to India by him were in such startling contradiction to what had gone before is a strong argument for their authenticity. Vigorous activity, the wish to mingle with the world in order to secure its salvation, self-confidence, a burning proselytism—these are uncommon aspects enough to constitute the solid foundation which legend has invested with the marvellous.

The man who was later on to be known as the Buddha—the Awakened or Enlightened one—was probably born some 556 years before our era, in the basin of the middle Ganges. In that region the river, swollen at Allahabad by the waters of the Jumna, veers in an easterly direction. It has then to flow past Benares before reaching Patna, the Pāṭaliputra of antiquity, where it drains the waters of the surrounding territories.

In the sixth century B.C. these were: to the east, Videha, with its capital Vaiśālī (now Bādar, in the district of Muzaffar-pur); north of the river the kingdom of Kosala, whose north-eastern

The Buddha with two disciples
(Pāla stele, Bengal work, 12th century).

15

*From the city of Kapilavastu, Prince Siddhārtha
could see the imposing landscapes of the Himalayas.*

tip belonged to the Śākya princes—today Oudh, on the borders of Nepal; and lastly, to the south, the whole great land of Magadha, the Bihār of modern times, whose capital was named Rājagṛha.

Buddhism arose, be it noted, to the east of where the river Sadānīrā descends from the frozen slopes of the Himalayas, in a region never penetrated by the fire-god Agni, and so in a land untouched at heart by Brahmanism; circumstances which allowed another mendicant order, that of the Jains, to spring up and thrive.

The kingdom, as it has pompously been styled, of the Śākyas was not even a principality of the Kosala kingdom, but at most the estate of a large landed proprietor. Provincial squires owning a fairly large stretch of land and living in a country seat which had at the same time to serve as a farm—such must the Śākyas have been, and such their palace. We should not forget that there flourished, not far from the residence of the Śākya chief, a wealthy capital—Kapilavastu, watered by the river Rohinī, still icy cold with snows from the northern mountains: a city which legend depicts as one of luxury.

*The market-towns of present-day Oudh may give an idea
of the domain of the Śākyas, large landed proprietors.*

It was several centuries after the Buddha's death that legend made a miracle of his birth. During the evenings men related how an archangel—a *bodhisattva*—was moved, as he looked upon earth from the height of the Tushita heaven, by the plight of human beings, gods and even demons. With the aim of saving them all, he sent his 'earthly reflection' into the womb of queen MĀYĀ, wife of the Śākya monarch, ŚUDDHODANA.

Māyā, who lived a life of strict austerity, and although thirty-two months married was Śuddhodana's wife in name only, had a strange premonition; so strange indeed and so intense that she could not make out, when she came to tell of it, if it were dream or reality. She found herself taken up to the heavens on a cloud, carried into an enchanted palace and finally approached by an elephant—described by some as a white one. With one of its six tusks the divine pachyderm pierced Māyā's side, without her feeling any pain. In this way the archangel had once again inserted his earthly reflection—the future Buddha—in the body of a woman who had already been his mother five hundred times: no god was adjudged worthy to be his father.

The birth took place, after a pregnancy of ten lunar months, in the park of Lumbinī, a pleasure-grove of King Śuddhodana sited some way from the capital. A shower of blossoms fell from the sky, the strains of heavenly music were heard and fly-whisks and parasols materialized in the air of their own accord as the infant emerged from his mother's right flank, without defilement, filled with learning and the remembrance of former lives.

We need not be astonished that he who was to become the Saviour of mankind should have chosen to be born in earthly wise: if, in fact, he had appeared out of the blue as Heaven's emissary men would certainly have despaired of ever being able to imitate him. By giving us an Indian-style account of the Annunciation, as well as of a gestation and a coming into the world without any organic contact with the mother, the Buddha's

The birth of Siddhartha. (Afghanistan.)

*The child Siddhārtha takes the seven steps towards
the cardinal points. (Tibetan painting.)*

biography (the *Lalita-vistara*) has merely prevented the character
of the birth from being exactly human.

Rising from the white lotus upon which his mother had laid
him, the new-born child surveyed space 'with the lion's glance'
and took seven steps towards each of the four cardinal points.
Then he spoke.

> I rank as the first in the world. I shall put an end to birth, to
> old age, to sickness and to death. Amongst all creatures I shall
> know no superior. . . . I am the chief in the world, I am the best
> in the world, I am the highest in the world. This is my last
> birth. There is now no other existence for me.

Striking the earth with his heel he declared,

> I shall vanquish the devil and the devil's army. For the sake
> of the beings immersed in hell and devoured by hell-fire I shall
> send down rain from the great cloud of the Law, and they shall
> be filled with joy and well-being.

Raising one finger towards the zenith he concluded, 'I shall
watch over all living beings!'

The seven steps, as de Lubac has stressed,[1] carry the Buddha-
to-be to the vault of the heavens. As soon as he is born he has
reached the 'Roof of the World' by traversing the seven cosmic
stages which correspond to the seven planetary heavens of

[1] See also Har Dayal, *Bodhisattva Doctrine*, p. 299.

Indian cosmogony. The Nativity myth gives expression in this way from the beginning to cosmic transcendance and the abolition of space and time.

Queen Māyā, being judged by the gods too sacred ever to give birth to any child, was recalled to their paradise at the end of seven days.

C. G. Jung points out that this sudden death of the mother (or the separation from her) forms part of the hero-mythos. The actual parent corresponds to the *anima virginale*, uncorrupted by the world and turned towards the sun, towards the transcendent whole in other words. Psychologically she represents the giving birth to a subconscious element, in the form of a child. The archetypal symbol of rebirth is projected on to the *adoptive* mother, who is sometimes an animal (the She-wolf of Romulus and Remus). In this case the part was played by Māyā's sister, who later married King Śuddhodana. The child was given the name SIDDHĀRTHA—'He who accomplishes'—and by this personal name and his patronymic Gautama he was known throughout his youth.

Shortly afterwards, his father was visited by a Himalayan ascetic who described to him the thirty-two marks which would one day appear on the body of the Buddha, in token of the destiny which awaited him.

There will be a protuberance on his skull; his hairs will curl towards the right in dark-blue locks; a small circle of silvery hairs will stand between his eyebrows on his wide, smooth forehead; his eyes, screened by lashes as long as a heifer's, will be large and very black; the lobes of his ears will be three times longer than usual; he will have forty sound and very even teeth, sheltering a long tapered tongue which will provide him with a keen sense of taste; his jaw will be as strong as that of a lion; he will have a fine, golden skin, a body as supple and firm as the stalk of the arum, a torso broad as the chest of a bull, even shoulders, well-rounded thighs, the legs of an antelope, and seven convex prominences; his hand will be broad; his arm, when hanging down, will touch his knee; and his very long fingers and toes will be joined by a fine membrane.

21

The hairs of his body will come forth individually, and those of his arms will turn upwards; his private member will be concealed; his heels will be fat and his palms smooth; a wheel with a thousand spokes will be drawn on the sole of each foot, and he will stand perfectly upright on his symmetrically equal feet; while his voice will sound like that of Brahmā.

He then went on to describe the eighty other, secondary marks: invisible veins, prominent copper-coloured nails, speech resembling the trumpeting of an elephant yet of a piercing sweetness, large heels, scarlet lips, lines of the hand deeply incised, etc.

Prince Siddhārtha grew up with the other young nobles of his own age, and always showed himself more than their match whether in archery, riding and swordsmanship, or in his knowledge of the sciences and of all known languages. There was not one Brahmin, nor one military instructor, who did not acknowledge when a few hours had passed that his pupil knew far more about it than he did himself.

King Śuddhodana, however,

Siddhārtha was as supreme in archery as in reading and recitation of texts. (Chinese painting on silk.)

was uneasy about a prediction that his son would become a great prince if he agreed to reign, but that if he ever adopted an ascetic's life he would be lost to the throne: for then he would pay no attention to anything but the salvation of all living creatures.

So the good monarch was overjoyed when Kṛishṇa, god of Love, pierced the prince's heart with an arrow for the fair GOPĀ YAŚODHARĀ: for surely a home, a ravishing wife one could not but cherish, and children would avert his mind from the ascetic ideal for ever?

Alas! Sweet as it was, Siddhārtha found the gilded idleness to which the king subjected him unbearable, and ventured into the city of Kapilavastu. Thrice were his eyes confronted with the harsh reality of life.

He met first an old man who bore upon his body the fearful ravages of eighty years. Another time he was drawn by the cries of a man afflicted with black plague of the groin. Then on the banks of the river he passed a procession of sobbing mourners on their way to the pyre with a corpse. Did the degradation of old age exist then, and sickness which reduces one to a howling

In the course of his four excursions Prince Siddhārtha met an aged beggar, a sick man, a corpse on its way to the pyre, a monk. These sights showed him the vanity of his princely life. (Chinese painting.)

animal, and death with its sad symphony of tears and lamentations? Must not each of us one day know such suffering? And is not that the inexorable price of merely being born?

It was in coming across a monk—a *bhikshu*—that the prince glimpsed the first stage of emancipation: and this was entirely in keeping with the Indian spirit. Thereupon Siddhārtha Gautama resolved to decline the crown, victory by the sword, and earthly glory. Out of love for men he would seek out Truth —a power stronger than that of the gods, who, after all, had never saved anyone from old age, sickness, affliction, and death. He was going to spend his whole life seeking a light still hidden from him, but which, he knew intuitively, would bring Deliverance to men.

Now came the 'Great Retirement'. Abandoning Gopā by night as she slept, renouncing every comfort of living, aided by gods who stifled every noise, he left his palace in silence. Plunging into the nearby forest, he stripped himself of his sumptuous clothing, cut off his hair, and, without turning back,

When Prince Siddhārtha left his sleeping palace, the gods placed their hands under the horse's shoes to avoid any noise. (Chinese painting on silk.)

The five yogis who, with Gautama, tried to find the Truth through asceticism and then deserted the Sage, were converted on hearing the Benares Sermon. (Borobuḍur, Java.)

set out alone in search of Truth. He was at that time twenty-nine years old.

For a long time he searched. On Vulture Peak, near the city of Rājagṛha, he came into contact with hermits practising the ascetic teachings of Udraka Rāmaputra, from whom he learnt to remain quite motionless, to control his breathing, and to 'fast like an insect during the bad season'. Under a yogin of the sāmkhya sect, ĀLĀRA KĀLĀMA, he discovered the vanity of these macerations, realizing that virtue is acquired neither through bodily pain nor by control of the senses.

Amongst the Brahmin priests who taught the quest for Ātman-Brahman, he found only involved beliefs and ready-made phrases without soul or sympathy. 'You do not care whether men become any better,' he declared when leaving them.

Truth, he decided, was something he would find within himself. Accompanied by five disciples whom he had met on the road, he retired into the district of Urubilva, not far from the city of Gayā, in central Bihār. For six years he was to meditate by the riverside, trying to further the refinement of his mind by ceasing to pay any attention to his body. Victory, consonant with the human condition, over the senses would correspond to the ascetic tradition of the yogins and represent the last stage to be passed before the attainment of sainthood.

It was not perfection which Gautama was seeking, however, but *gnosis*, or at any rate some key. Since there was still no sign of the knowledge he desired, and his reason was even losing

25

some of its edge, he resolved to live a more normal life and began regularly going to the village to beg food, holding out his bowl without a word and giving no thanks.

Garbed in a winding-sheet culled from a tomb, which he cut up and sewed to make himself a robe and a sash, Siddhārtha Gautama resumed the path to Gayā, surprising the peasants with the halo of light which surrounded him. He seemed unconscious of the magical aspect assumed by the countryside about, and had no ears for the celestial strains which set the atmosphere a-quiver. He did not know where he was going, but guessed that he was drawing near to the Tree of Knowledge.

He halted, when night fell, at the foot of a fig-tree, and knew that he had arrived. He never for a second doubted that he would meet in this place, not the peace which comes with meditation, but the supreme revelation which till now he had pursued without success.

He only turned from contemplation of the fig-tree to accept eight armfuls of mowing grass offered him by a stupefied reaper. Then, having walked seven times round the tree in salutation, he stopped to the east of it, arranged the heap of grass as a seat, and sat down cross-legged—in the lotus position. 'Were my skin to dry up, my hand to wither, and my bones to dissolve, until I have attained to supreme and absolute knowledge I shall not stir from this seat.'

With his tongue thrust against his palate, one hand touching the earth to summon it to witness and to be penetrated by its effluvia, Gautama 'restrained, crushed and racked' his mind. Seeing him thus determined, Māra, lord of sensory pleasures, left the celestial throne from which he ruled over the six lower levels of heaven, and over earth and hell. Much like Lucifer before the fall, he was a deity of the highest rank, and by birth he was stationed immediately below Brahmā himself.

Māra was afraid. If men ever came to be set free by what this saint had to offer them, would not this leave him, Māra, a commander without an army, a sovereign without subjects? The meditator must be put to flight then. But in vain did he unleash hurricane, thunderbolt and torrents of rain: nothing could disturb one fold of Gautama's robe, nothing could interfere with his ecstasy.

In the course of the first watch of the night, the Sage became acquainted with everything that had taken place in his earlier lives; the middle watch showed him the present condition of the universe; and before dawn brought the third watch to an end he had mastered the whole chain of cause and effect. Two Truths had burst upon him.

How miserable, then, is this world! A world which grows old and dies only to be reborn, and grow old and die again and again without cease. But is not the cause of this growing old and of this dying birth, and the desire of birth?

And so, from cause to cause, he traced the line to ignorance, the cause of erroneous attitudes. At last, the final thought flashed forth:

By killing desire, which leads from birth to birth, new births and new woes will be prevented. There is no other means to kill this desire than to lead a pure life.

Four weeks went by while the Buddha, without leaving his seat of grass, toured the world. Māra tried to reduce him to a human plane by sending him the customary temptations offered to ascetics. Being also a god of Love, he dispatched three of his most seductive daughters to dance before the Enlightened one, named Lust, Restlessness, and Greed. A single glance from the Sage withered their beauty in a moment.

Foiled again, the King of Hell used his last weapon: he confronted the Buddha with the enormity of the task of salvation, and suggested that, now the cause of human sorrow had been found, he leave men to make the best they could of it, and obtain Nirvāna here and now by bringing his last stay on earth to an end. He had touched on a sensitive spot: the Sage really did hesitate to divulge his revelation—for fear of not being understood, of being unable to translate the inexpressible into words, and perhaps of seeing his ideas travestied.

For in this point the Buddha was destined to fail. Holy books

Māra, god of sensory desires, the earth, and hell tries to turn the Buddha from his mission by sending his daughters to dance before the Enlightened one. (Borobudur, Java.)

written several centuries after the Enlightenment wilfully ignore the Sage's negative attitude towards Brahman, and, careless of contradiction, inform us that he needed all the help of the Universal Breath to maintain his composure.

With his finger-tips the Enlightened one touched the piece of ground where he had been meditating, and which Māra wished to recapture from him: had he not gained by innumerable acts of self-sacrifice in his former lives the right to watch over the whole of the earth? His mind was made up from that instant: balancing the eternal peace of Nirvāṇa against the love he bore to men, he preferred to become a Buddha for everyone and to wait until the deliverance of mankind was accomplished.

In May, when the monsoon set in, his meditation was not at an end. For seven days at a stretch the rain lashed down, an icy hurricane hurled itself upon the earth, and darkness covered the sky. In spite of Māra, MUCILINDA, king of the Nāgas, raised the Sage up on his coils above the waters, and spread out his seven heads to protect him from the tempest. Then when calm had returned, he loosed his coils and assumed the form of a resplendent young man paying his adorations to the Blessed one.

The Buddha did not overlook the fact that only the first part of the mission he took upon himself, by deciding to live through one last earthly existence, had thus been fulfilled. None the less, having grasped the Truth, he felt some apprehension when called upon to proclaim it to the world: a Truth which was 'profound, difficult to perceive, hard to know, transcending all thought, only to be grasped by the wise'.

What can it serve to reveal to the world what I have gained in these painful strivings? The Truth is not easily learnt by those beset with lust and hatred. It is something which costs trouble, full of mystery, profound, and hidden from the coarser spirit: he whose mind is veiled in darkness by earthly desires is unable to see it.

Pondering to whom he should first teach his word of salvation, he thought of the five disciples who had abandoned him when he broke his fast. He knew he would find them at Benares since, of course, he knew everything.

On the way he met one of his earliest masters, Upaka, and introduced himself for the first time as saint and victor—*Arhat* and *Jina*. But he did not disclose any of the Doctrine to him, reserving it for a better audience. Continuing on his way, he reached the banks of the Ganges, which he crossed miraculously through the air.

When at last he rejoined the five monks, he confined himself to telling them with the utmost simplicity, 'I am the Saint, the Perfect one, the Fully Enlightened. Give ear, O monks: the way is found. Hear me.'

Prostrating themselves before

Mucilinda, king of the Nāgas, raises the Sage above the waters and protects him with his seven heads.

The Preaching of the Buddha.

this apparition of light which they sensed to be far mightier than any of the gods they had hitherto worshipped, the monks listened—more with the heart than with the ear—to the revelation now known as the SERMON AT BENARES ('Sūtra of Setting in Motion the Wheel of the Doctrine').

> Learn, O monks, that all existence is naught but pain: inasmuch as death, contact with what one does not like, separation from what one likes or the inability to satisfy one's desires, are painful. . . . The origin of this universal pain is the craving to exist, the craving for the pleasures of the five external senses and the internal sense, and even the craving to die.

His words pierced the monks like darts, but far from hurting them they flooded them with joy. Even antelopes had come, enchanted, to listen to the wondrous sermon, and laid their cool muzzles against the Blessed one's cheek.

> What, O monks, is the Middle Way, which the Tathāgata has discovered, which gives sight to the mind, which tends to calm, to insight, to enlightenment and to Nirvāna?

Learn first that it lies between the extremes of asceticism and the worldly life. Know next that it is an Eightfold path, whose divisions are named perfect Beliefs, perfect Resolve, perfect Speech, perfect Action, perfect Living, perfect Effort, perfect Remembrance and perfect Meditation.

This, O monks, is the noble Truth of pain. . . .

This, O monks, is the noble Truth of the ending of pain. . . .

This, O monks, is the noble Truth of the way that leads to the ending of pain, a path serene and free.

This, O monks, is the noble Truth of the eight right activities which are unaffected by the desire of the desirable or by the fear of the formidable.

Then with the point of his stick the Buddha drew the Wheel of Existence in the dust, the *Kāla-cakra* which with its twelve stages is clasped in the fangs of Impermanence.

The Wheel contains the Gods in their heaven, men, animals, and the inhabitants of hell. And until it attaches itself to the centre for all eternity, the spark which vitalises every living body goes from one sector to another according to its actions. Remember this well: do not rebel against your present condition, for it is a punishment for the past. Know also that your future destiny depends upon your purity of heart. That which I teach you is the Law of Karman.

Nearly forty-five years of evangelization now went down in the history of the world. To follow the Buddha in his comings and goings is rather difficult, although they were confined to the north-eastern corner of India: Nepal, Bihar, and Oudh. He and his disciples would halt during the season of the monsoon rains, from June to September, when the hot summer downpours turned the roads into quagmires and so prevented open-air preaching.

It was not as a pilgrim who had made a name for himself, or as a yogin far wiser, holier and more devoted to mankind than any known before, that the Enlightened one was received. He was neither yogin nor pilgrim, but the Saviour of man, and no name was any longer apposite. The faithful addressed him as 'Master', and only referred to him by the use of epithets: the

Worthy (*Arhat*), the Perfect, the Genuinely Arrived (*Tathāgata*), He whose Name is Truth (*Satyanāman*, Pāli *Saccanāma*), the Blessed, the Lord (*Bhagavat*), the Unfathomable (Pāli *Anoma*). He was even named He-who-has-become-Dharma to express his identification with the Eternal Law he expounded.

It was not the common herd that the Buddha sought to enlighten. He frankly acknowledged that millennial traditions, superstition, a liking for magic and, not least, their submission to the Brahmins, had firmly walled in the understanding of the humble folk. As a Kshatriya, he was more anxious to inculcate his teaching in the *élite*, the warrior nobility, who were politically rather anti-clerical. The Brahmins had little love for him, as may be imagined, for he denied their utility as mediators between man and his salvation. However, they were almost alone in their hostility to him; for the common people of India, even if they did not follow his teaching very well, were not without some inkling of the stupendous dawn of a new conception of existence. The Buddha himself was mild and compassionate-natured, and lost his patience only once: on that occasion a Brahmin, Kaśyapa of Uruvelā, claimed to be his superior in sainthood. For his benefit the Perfect one pronounced what has since been named the FIRE-SERMON.

> The fire of life must be put out [he thundered]. For everything in the world is on fire with the fire of lust, the fire of hatred, and the fire of illusion. Birth, old age, death, care, lamentation, pain, sorrow and despair are so many flames. . . . The impressions received by your eye, Brahmin, are on fire; the impressions received by your ear are on fire. And it is the same for your five senses, and your internal sense.
>
> Are you not then disgusted by your senses, by the sense-objects, the impressions and the feelings which they provoke? If you are disgusted, then know that you are delivered, free from passions. And understand, Brahmin, that birth is ended for you and that this true sainthood of which you spoke is about to be achieved. All the rest is but an illusion, which devours you like a flame.

Opposition there was, but it always swiftly yielded before the

The Buddha and the three Kāśyapa brothers.
(Afghanistan.)

32

profundity of the Master's words. Hostile Brahmins such as the three Kaśyapa brothers gave in when they witnessed the stupendous miracles that the Buddha performed as if it were child's play. Disciples wearing the yellow robe thronged about him ready to continue his work, including the Brahmin ŚĀRIPUTRA, MAUDGALYĀYANA, and many others whose names the scriptures have carefully preserved for us. Monarchs lent him their support: e.g., PRASENAJIT, King of Kosala, and BIMBISĀRA, King of Magadha.

From the royal family of the Śākyas downwards the entire population was converted when the Sage, yielding to the earnest appeals of the old king Śuddhodana, returned to Kapilavastu after an absence of thirty-five years. The aunt who had reared him, his wife Gopā, Rāhula the son he had never known, and all the princes bowed their heads to him who taught that we are subjected to illusion, and that everything is paid for in full.

No transgression can be redeemed. Man is born alone, lives alone and dies alone; and it is he alone who can blaze the trail which leads him to Nirvāna, the wondrous realm of non-being and non-becoming.

He developed his theme at some length, tracing the implacable wheel of life, the Kālacakra, evoking the faceless, feelingless power which rules the workings of the world, and propounding the Four Truths with which he had been illumined. Then, looking down upon the multitude, he gave them some human advice.

These are the five rules of your everyday life. Be compassionate and respect even the most lowly form of life. Give and receive freely but take nothing that is not given. Never lie, even on occasions which seem to you to justify falsehood. Avoid drugs and drink. Respect woman, and commit no illicit and unnatural carnal act.

Years went by. The disciples, thousands of them already, were organized in communities. Thus, they travelled about spreading the doctrine or lived, in the monsoon season, in *vihāras*—huts made of branches, or modest wooden houses given by princes, sited at once far enough from and near enough to the cities: far enough for the bustle of city life to leave their meditations undisturbed, yet near the suburbs, so that rich benefactors might take an interest in the community, and the Blessed one—the Bhagavat—come with his numerous entourage to preach to them.

It was the year 476 before Christ, and Śākyamuni was by now eighty years old, but age seemed to have no hold over him.

Still, his time was undoubtedly at an end, for suddenly the Buddha fell ill when on his way to Kuśinagara (Pāli *Kusinārā*), capital of the Malla State. At the first shivers that laid him low he knew that the moment had come for picked disciples to receive his last instructions.

He smiled as Ānanda carefully prepared his master's couch. 'Maitreya too,' he presently remarked, 'the next Buddha, who will come to earth thousands of years from now to perfect my work, will have his own Ānanda.'

He seated himself in the lotus position, weary in body but more lucid in spirit than ever. The yellow robes thronged about him, old men who for twenty years had been able to fathom all the subtlety of his thoughts and still dizzy youths not altogether detached from the world. Some peasants from the village had mingled with the austere assembly out of curiosity.

For the last time the Buddha was about to speak; summarizing his teaching, as found in the 'Triple Basket' (*Tri-piṭaka*)—the name given to the canonical books handed down to us as assembled by his disciples.

In all the universes, visible and invisible, there exists but one single force, without beginning or end, without any law but its own, without preference or aversion. It kills and it saves with no other aim than the working out of Destiny. Death and Pain are the shuttles of its loom, Love and Life are the threads.

But do not try to measure the Immeasurable with words, nor seek with the aid of the plummet of thought to sound the unfathomable: he who asks is deluded, and he who answers is deluded.

Expect nothing from pitiless Gods, themselves subject to the law of Karma, who are born, grow old and die only to be reborn, and have not succeeded in throwing off their own woe. Expect all from yourself: nor forget that each can gain a power greater than that of Indra himself.

Tears were trickling down Ānanda's cheeks, and the Master raised a finger of reproof: 'After all that I have taught you, how can you still feel grief? Is it so hard then for a man to get rid of all suffering?'

And with a certain weariness at the difficulty mankind could experience in breaking out of its matrix, he went on:

Do not let yourself be deceived, Ānanda. Life is a long agony, it is only pain: and the child is right to cry as soon as he is born. That is the First Truth.

The Second Truth is that pain comes only from Desire. Man clings desperately to shadows; he becomes infatuated with dreams, sets up a false 'I' in the centre, and builds an imaginary world around it. When his soul forsakes him, it will depart saturated with the poisons he has drunk; and then be reborn with a burning desire to drink anew.

The Third Truth is the possible ending of pain. You will only obtain it, Ānanda, by triumphing over all the attachments to which you are subject and by tearing from your heart any passions that may still remain there. Then you will live higher than the Gods.

But listen well to this Fourth Truth, which is the eightfold Path of Salvation. First become aware of the Karman which shapes your future destiny. Then, have only feelings that are free from malevolence, greed and wrath. Next, watch over your lips as if they were the gates of a king's palace: nothing impure must leave them. And lastly, let each of your actions be directed against a fault, or assist a merit to increase. Those are the first four divisions of the Path. Do you not agree that any man could follow these four courses?

Then [concluded the Master], once you have annihilated egoism, false belief, doubt, hatred and greed, and are reborn, then you can follow, in your new existence, the other four courses which bear the names of right Purity, right Thought, right Solitude, and right Ecstasy. By then you will automatically be in a position to conquer your desire to live on earth, your desire to go to heaven, your errors, and last but not least your pride in having advanced along the road of sainthood. You will be near indeed to Nirvāna.

When he felt the cold reach his stomach, Gautama stretched himself out a little. Refusing help with a wave of the hand, he kept by him only those he judged worthy to carry out his work: their feet had been wounded, and then strengthened, on the stony path of Virtue. To these he recalled the ten prohibitions, the principles of the Order, the rules of everyday life, clothing, and food, the method of meditation, and the danger involved in 'skipping' stages.

There will before long be five hundred million believers following the Law. Taking refuge therein, I leave you.

The last words he spoke were to show the nullity of the things we think must really exist:

When at the age of eighty years the Buddha passed away amidst his disciples, his mission of salvation accomplished, he entered Nirvāna, delivered for ever from rebirths. (Grèco-Buddhist work from Gandhāra.

Behold the body of the Tathāgata. All compound things are subject to decay. Work out your end with diligence.

Then he lay down on his right side and sank into meditation, whilst a sublime melody descended from the sky. No one could tell at what moment the Buddha passed from ecstasy to deliverance in Nirvāna, where everlasting silence dwells.

Before long it was being told how marvellous events accompanied the last rites of one who, already honoured as an envoy of heaven, had just died as a man amongst men. The air became luminous, and music coming from nowhere flooded the ears of those present. The pyre on which the Master's corpse was to be cremated burst into spontaneous flames and afterwards went out all at once, while the scent of jasmine filled the air.

A war would have broken out to decide which of several kings should have custody of the ashes: elephants were decked out for war, archers manned the city walls, and cavalry scoured the countryside. The gathering storm was quelled by the mediation of a Brahmin, who said: 'Seven stūpas forty cubits high shall be built in the territories of the seven kings to receive the relics. And the eighth part of the ashes shall be entrusted to the seven-headed Nāga serpents, in the heart of the forest.'

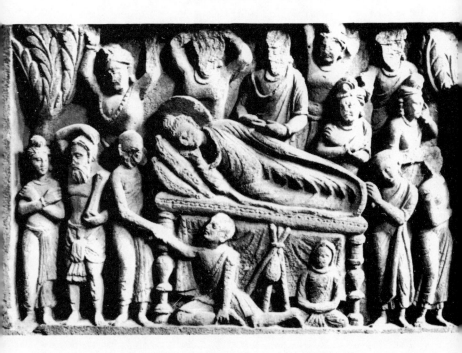

THE OLD SCHOOL OF WISDOM

THE BUDDHIST DOCTRINE

> The Buddha can only tell you
> the way: it is for you yourself to
> make the effort.—DHAMMAPADA.

Through our study of pre-Buddhist India and our summary of the legendary life of Gautama we have already glimpsed the outlines of the doctrine the Buddha preached. We shall presently be able to point out some of its more essential features. The reader should not, however, imagine that he will find its structure balanced and logical in its sequence and progressions, or, in a word, Cartesian. Although it has spread far beyond the bounds of the peninsula, the doctrine was conceived in India, and, from the third century before to the seventh century after Christ, was edited and modified by Indian brains, so that its lack of precision is not deliberate but generic. At every turn of phrase, the varied meanings which words may be assigned lead to ambiguity. Since, apart from this, the interpretation given by individual Buddhist scholars is liable to variation, it is plain that we Westerners run the risk of losing our foothold on such shaky ground.

That, however, does not appear to incommode Buddhists in the East: they find all the more profundity in Śākyamuni's teachings for his having left their comprehension so much scope. And still more than what was formulated in this way do they value the silence maintained by the Buddha upon certain points.

And one last important remark: it is not possible for us to distinguish the *real* teaching laid down by the Buddha from that authorized by the councils. We *cannot* rely upon the authenticity of the words attributed to Śākyamuni, any more than we can picture his appearance and manner of life. We do not know whether he was short or tall; bearded, vehement or restrained; and we have no trustworthy evidence of what he said and did.

The Buddha explains the Doctrine to his disciples.
(Indian work from Amaravāti.)

The only tradition that can be vouched for is that he existed and that he produced a new doctrine.

For the rest we can only trust to his commentators—none of whom wrote in the Master's lifetime: all they did was to 'fix' an already lengthy sequence of oral transmissions by writing it down. And there again it must be supposed that historical Buddhism is not exactly the same as primitive Buddhism: cross-checking makes it possible to observe very appreciable differences.

Perhaps the original Buddhism was purely rational and agnostic, a discipline offered as a tribute to the spiritual possibilities of man. It would only have been later on that scholars introduced ideas in contradiction with the primitive concepts, e.g. that of the Non-self, monasticism, a luxuriant mythology and all the ritual of worship. But must the Buddhism of the year 500 B.C. really curtail our vision of that—of those, rather—which flourished in the course of later centuries? Where roses bloom, must the sweet briar alone engross attention?

If in the present work the author has sought to approximate to the original Doctrine whenever there was any solid indication to go by, he has never felt it of any use to assert the orthodoxy of this Doctrine when comparing various theories, sometimes startlingly at variance with it.

Origins of the Doctrine: The DHARMA (doctrine) naturally stems from man's ancient attempts to control the world during his lifetime, and to secure immortality after his death. Pressing the matter further than the old wisdoms, perhaps, it forbore to define the kingdom of the spirit but studied some of the methods by which it is to be attained:

(*a*) a reappraisal, amounting to negation, of sense-experience;

(*b*) a renunciation of all attachment;

(*c*) allowance for the equality of all creation;

(*d*) refusal to consider anything whatsoever as stable and permanent.

The Doctrine, then, is not in essence a dogma—or a group of dogmata—but, rather, a way, a psychological attitude, a reference to certain views about the universe. It is a stern discipline, of course; but as a means to attain salvation, not as an end to which self-mastery is directed.

Of whatever teachings you can assure yourself that they conduce to dispassion and not to passions; to detachment and not to bondage; to decrease of worldly gains and not to their increase; to frugality and not to covetousness; to content and not to discontent; to solitude and not to company; to energy and not to sloth; to delight in good and not in evil; of these teachings you may declare with certainty: this is the norm, this is the discipline, this is the Master's message.

It seems clear that the Doctrine was built upon foundations long accepted by the yogins. The earth and mankind were of little account to these ascetics: the knowledge which mattered was that of the worlds above and below, heavens and hells, invisible to the common man. This was not a question of the imaginary, but on the contrary of a fantastic, hidden, spatial fact about the universe. Such Knowledge, which for the yogins took on a mystical application, a philosophical and moral turn, was built up on the basis of suprasensory perceptions. To discover the structure of the invisible worlds was tantamount to having control over Nature: with the double aim of obtaining deliverance and of practising the art of magic on other people.

But the yogins themselves, with their beatific vision of the Absolute, represented only one landmark in a world of spiritual methods and ideas peculiar to the East. It is undeniable in fact that, while the European mind was still groping in darkness, Asia—and India in particular—already had a long acquaintance with the quest for the spiritual.

ABHI-DHARMA, or extended Dharma, is simply the division (*piṭaka*) of that name in the Buddhist scriptural canon: it is devoted to scholastic elaboration of the Doctrine set forth in the *Sūtra-piṭaka*. This turns out to be the most heterogeneous mixture imaginable. It draws upon all systems, and juxtaposes their disparate elements with nothing in common but the three keys: lofty Morality, contemplative Meditation, and psychological Wisdom.

41

We find traces of the old Vedānta, for instance, so far as the latter can be made out, in certain Brāhmaṇas and Upanishads: its theories of Name and Form have been borrowed for metaphysics. From yoga the Doctrine took over the rules to be observed in philosophical meditation. In method and terminology, the dharma is indebted to medicine for its diagnosis of the ills of this world: the conception of the five *skandhas* (either 'Components' or 'Aggregates': body, feelings, perceptions, inpulses and emotions, and acts of consciousness) is curiously dependent on anatomy.

Though these facts have to be recorded, they contain, after all, nothing that need astonish us. No remarkable difference can be found between Jainism and the mystical theology of Catholicism, or between the asceticism of the Stylite Christian hermits of Egypt and the disciplines of Buddhism. There exists a kind of oneness in the search for salvation, and the systems are basically comparable.

It may be acknowledged then that Buddhism inherited a part of its spiritual aspirations from Brahmanism. What is peculiar to it is the authority given to man to gain his salvation without divine intervention. The ground had already been prepared by the fall of the old Vedic gods, which proved that a place in the celestial empyrean was not held in perpetuity. A Nietzschean before Nietzsche, the Buddha might well have uttered the axiom 'The gods are dead, man grows.' He attaches so much importance to the individual as to state outright that in order to gain Nirvāṇa even the gods must undergo their last incarnation in the human state.

Yet when we study its psychological pragmatism and its theory of salvation by Release more closely, we observe that apart from a few points in common with Brahmanism (dissatisfaction with human imperfection, transmigration), Buddhism has broken with the concepts of its time, concerning the non-human world.

For instance the Buddha never referred to Brahman, the unique and impersonal divine entity. He paid no attention to the Ātman, and so could not envisage a return into the womb of the supreme Being. The Brahmins denied the reality of the world around us, and the only reality they recognized was the Ātman; for the Buddhists it was Suffering, and its origin Desire.

For them, since Deliverance was well-defined and within everyone's reach, there was no need of those intermediaries between man and the divine, the Brahmins. Whilst it is true that the idea of *karman* persisted, it was no longer subject to rites but depended on the 'net total' of one's own deeds. There was no need therefore for either ceremonies or formulae, a conviction which eliminated the privileged Brahmin caste, hereditary custodian of the Vedic tradition. The sacrifice of animals became a sin in Buddhism, which recognized as valid only the sacrifice of all to which man is attached.

In this sense Buddhism, compared with the ideas then current, does represent an innovation, firmly based though it is on previous contributions. Whereas Brahmanism was a closed, traditionally cultured, specifically Indian egocentric religion, Buddhism presented itself as a universal spiritual aspiration, practised according to disciplines in which the divine had no part: its decline in Brahmanic India and its expansion in the Asian world were to be expected.

Gautama was justifiably apprehensive about the strength of popular belief in the efficacy of ceremonies. He fought such beliefs, but never succeeded in wiping them out completely enough not to be restored again one day, more vigorous than ever. 'The common people,' he would say, 'the ignorant and the women are poorly gifted in understanding. They remain attached to base superstitions and to the promptings of sensibility,' precisely that subjective sensibility which he wished to root out.

Buddhism has been credited with the suppression of the Brahmanic castes. This only happened as a consequence of the fact that the Dharma placed man on a spiritual plane far above all social segregation: it did not aim merely at the salvation of the Indian but at that of every man. When Buddhism had to yield to a revival of Brahmanism (Hinduism), the division into castes reappeared tighter than ever.

There has been talk of the Buddhist pessimism about suffering (as distinct from the Brahmanist pessimism which concerns itself with impurity): I shall return to this farther on, but let it be made clear here and now that the Dharma is much less despairing than is supposed—after all, one need only call to mind the extraordinary serenity of its adepts. The Doctrine formally rejects the fearful burden of predestination, as it does the individual's conception and birth in sin. Far from being a final product of nature, man with his faults and merits is entitled to consider the vastest horizons of spiritual improvement open to him. Since a beginning which we are unable to envisage (not because of the time which divides us from it but through the inconceivability of 'something' arising out of 'nothing') man has evolved and will continue to evolve: not as a human mass, but individual by individual.

Without dwelling here on karman, let us merely remember that man is reborn according to his deeds, and that he is master of his fate—as soon, at least, as he has realized the necessity of deliverance. The Doctrine is designed to help him free himself on the psychological and moral planes. Its developments, its recommendations, and the asceticism of the formula of life which it offers are only, after all, an aid. The great news which the Buddha brought, 'Give ear, the release from death is found', is supplemented by a call to self-reliance: 'every man shapes his own destiny' was the Buddhist creed.

Dharma and the Divine: When we speak of divinity the word 'religion' comes naturally to mind. And this word at once involves us, as far as Buddhism is concerned, in a hazardous question. Are we dealing with a religion? Reference is here made, of course, to pure Buddhism, and not to the changes which love of the supernatural has inflicted on it in the course of twenty-five centuries.

The answer is less simple than it seems. Suffice it to give the opinion of two eminent Burmese Buddhists, formulated at the 'Wesak' celebrations in 1952:

The venerable Bhikshu U Thittila: 'The Buddha's teaching is not a religion but a practical mode of living.'

His Highness Maung Ji: 'Buddhism is a democratic religion, and one day will perhaps be the world religion, because you find in it the equality of all men.'

But he, no doubt, was disregarding forms of worship, and giving the word *religion* the sense of a spiritual bond binding the adepts.

In any case all theistic expressions and all theology must be banished from our remarks about the Dharma, since they would give a false impression of it.

The attitude to the divine is easier to state. The Buddha did not condemn any divinity, any cult, or even the belief in powers higher than man: he ignored them as irrelevant to his teaching.

We know that he accepted gods, but as beings placed temporarily above the human sphere and subject to the same fate as we—if not worse. The Blessed one also spoke of hell, but as a series of unpleasant places of punishment, their character not ultimately distinguishable from that of any paradise. That was the interpretation offered to the less advanced; for others, hells and heavens were individual states of consciousness—a way of thinking that cannot but remind us of Sartre's *Huit-Clos*.

There is therefore no possibility of 'redemption', nor of course any Redeemer on whom, as on the scapegoat of old, are loaded all the sins of the world. The round of rebirths (Samsāra) alone exists, and from it, as we shall shortly see, the soul (psyche) is wholly lacking.

In his conversation with Sudatta, the Buddha makes it quite clear that he excluded the creation of the universe by Iśvara from his concerns. For him, it was proven fact that the gods themselves were incapable of salvation without, first, passing through the state of men, nay more, the state of men who have adopted the monastic life (*Bhikshus*). It was hence of no interest that transmigration might at one point bring the individual to the state of a god, since that was only a pleasant but transitory stage. The Sage, in any case, called himself 'teacher of gods and men'.

The attainment of a saint's condition, on the other hand,

turned out to be advantageous, because irreversible. After sainthood, the path of final release lay wide open. The Buddha had been a saint before knowing Enlightenment; there and then, he was a saint no more, and a man in appearance only: he was the first recipient of Nirvāna.

We shall see in later chapters that there exist a lower and a higher Doctrine, the one suitable for laymen and the other constituting a metaphysic and a discipline proper to monks living in a community and to recluses. The lower Doctrine is a natural preparation for the monastic dharma: a pure life and pure thoughts. That 'the person who desires truth, has compassion for the outcasts of fortune and con-

The lotus rising unsoiled above the waters represents supreme purity radiating over the world. (Chinese painting.)

trols his lusts and anger, has understood the two worlds' is within the reach of the most rudimentary understanding. But, developed, it can bring about deliverance.

The portion of the teachings set within reach of the most backward of men takes the form of a moral code. What distinguishes it from codes contingent on anthropomorphic deities armed with commands and prohibitions, is that it rests on the solid law of causality, applicable to every living thing and not only to man. The exhortation to a 'free' but unflinching morality, without any other speculation, is so straightforward that the simple adepts invited to follow it saw in the Buddha a smiling 'Good Lord', come down from Heaven to help men. For the believer the ideal was to find, in his turn, a place within the Buddhist lotus, symbol of radiant purity.

THE DOCTRINE OF SUFFERING

The Buddha's whole doctrine is based on his discovery of human suffering. There indeed was innovation: Brahmanism had never felt that transmigration was linked with everlasting recurrence, or that the fact of existing represented in itself the pitiless price of belonging to the world, whether earth, or heaven, or hell.

There is not the least likelihood that the Master attached a metaphysical sense to what was only—as everyone could see for himself—a sad statement of fact. With precision Gautama demonstrated to men (who had not perhaps suspected it till then) that birth is at the origin of all pain. Is it not painful that a fair young body should succumb in the end to decrepitude or disease, painful to lose what one has taken so much trouble to gain or what is so dear to you emotionally, to see what one desires remain always out of reach, or to lean upon what one thinks stable and permanent when ceaseless change plunges us at every moment into error? And to end it all, death, death with that frightful prospect that all is not ended even then.

Vedism spoke of a region where human beings were rewarded or punished. Brahmanism had based itself on transmigration,

with the chance of managing, during a given incarnation, to dissolve one's Ātman in the universal Brahman. No one had centred the problem on the vital fact: every rebirth entails its sum of pain. Whether it be worse or better than before is secondary; life is bad in itself.

Man easily forgets his numberless disappointments to cling to the rare joys he can extract from life. Only when his body plays him false, or he faces death, does he see the vanity of his existence. It is too late! He has made poor use of his sojourn on earth, and the spark which animates his perishable body must once more find some being as a support. Happy such a man, if the new condition is not worse than its predecessor, in punishment for past misdeeds!

The Buddha had therefore to show men that life is much less good than they suppose it to be. Then, in investigating a topic which had already been established in India before his time, he was not content to open men's eyes: he had to influence their understanding. That is why he set about representing human misery as having a deeper character than the griefs, disappointments, gaps or deficiencies that are visible. It was incertitude that he found in it, the spiritual anguish (*duhkha*), the inescapable decay of everything created (*anitya*) and the illusion (*anātman*) on which humanity feeds. Having thus painted the true picture of suffering, he dissected its mechanism.

The first cause of pain is DESIRE. Although it was the green snake of lechery that he drew in the centre of the Wheel of Life, the Master had not solely carnal desires in view, but all possessiveness, all eagerness to attempt, to win and to keep.

The second cause of suffering is no other than LACK OF SELF-CONTROL. The red cock does not symbolize Wrath alone; he stands for the surrender to passions and feelings. How lowering it is for man not to be able to resist attacks of temper, immoderation of language, and the fallacious pleasures of good food, dancing, or gaming! To give way to them is to become their slave, or think only of the gratifications experienced. To strike a person who insults you; to gossip thoughtlessly; to anticipate the delights of the palate by sniffing the dish one is

The Wheel of Life. (Dharmacakra).
Centre, the three causes of pain;
Intermediate, the six possible states of rebirth;
Outer ring, the twelve stages of human existence;
Encircling the wheel, Impermanence. (Sino-Tibetan painting.)   49

about to be served—all prevent us from facing the real problem, viz. that blow calls forth counter-blow, or other reprisal; that judgement is never justified, since no one possesses all the data of a case; that satiety soon comes with the best meal and that the best meal results in a noisome product; that gambling, dancing, music and good company deflect your being from the true path, which is *to know*.

And this leads quite naturally to the third cause, which is IGNORANCE—or rather the refusal or disregard of knowledge. The Buddha did not blame the humble for being poor in spirit; but he revealed to them, as he did to those who possess the faculty of thought, the terrible danger of not seeking to know, of wilfully or heedlessly ignoring the fact that earthly life is but a sorry tissue: the few gilded spangles of short-lived joys do not succeed in making it iridescent. Nothing expresses this apathy better than the pallid Hog of Ignorance. Snout in the ground, he is only concerned with the matter in hand, heedless of the sky above him. 'In the vortex of Becoming, the impermanence, decay and death of all that has had a beginning are inevitable: to live or to become is a function of feeling; to feel is a function of desire; and to desire is a function of ignorance' (Coomaraswamy). Thus ignorance is tantamount to an original sin, and represents the primal source of all suffering and servitude.

Later on the commentators were to personify our attachment to the vain pleasures of this world by setting the figure of Māra against that of the Liberator. Māra is much less the Fiend, the Evil one, the Devil, than, rather, Life itself.

In each sermon and each conversation the Buddha returns to the pain of existence, and to the causes of this suffering. He frequently dwells on the harmful illusion of thinking what is impermanent to be fixed, of relying on appearances which have nothing to do with reality—if a reality even exists. In this he is at one with the Upanishads, which held that the 'experiential' personality (Jīva) and the perceptible world (nature, matter: *prakṛti*) are mere appearances and no more.

Behind suffering, growing old and illusion stands the inconstancy of all that we believe permanent. There is nothing created which is not already on the way to disappearance: 'Instantaneous is the annihilation of all life.' If the Buddha had been an anatomist he would have cited as an example the living body, in which millions of cells are destroyed each second and replaced by new ones; and the individual who wakes up is not the same who lay down to sleep the night before.

But contempt for existence was only justified if new prospects were offered to counterbalance it. The original Buddhism banished metaphysics to the domain of the unknowable with determined agnosticism, and directed itself rationally towards a solution within everybody's reach. Of the ruthless exposure of pain, it only retained as much as would be of practical service for the attainment of happiness wherever it can be found.

> Looking for the maker of this tabernacle, I have run through a course of many births, not finding him; and painful is birth again and again. But now, maker of the tabernacle, thou hast been seen; thou shalt not make up this tabernacle again. All thy rafters are broken, thy ridge-pole is sundered; the mind, approaching the Eternal [freedom from all composite things] has attained to the extinction of all desires. (*Dhammapada*, tr. M. Müller.)

When his disciple Mālunkyāputta expressed indignation that the Doctrine did not deal with the origin of world-systems or a possible after-life, the Buddha declared:

> The knowledge of all these things cannot advance one a single step on the road of sainthood and peace. I have come to teach you what serves these purposes: the truth about suffering, its causes and its extinction.

It must not be supposed that the conception of life on earth as bad by nature was hailed with enthusiasm. The Buddha was not mistaken when he said:

> It is difficult to shoot arrow after arrow through a narrow keyhole at a distance, and not once miss. It is more difficult to pierce with the tip of a hair split a hundred times another sliver

of hair similarly split. But it is infinitely more difficult yet to grasp that all that exists, being subject to or causing pain, is evil.

The masses readily reconciled themselves to a present existence, and even the prospect of future existences, which they found, after all, fairly pleasant. They did not by any means feel tired of being reborn, and had no ambition to be released from their rebirths. The Buddha's great compassion towards human beings, such as one might have for children who think themselves happy, met with haughty opposition from the men: since gods, animals, women and even monks had to be born one last time in a man's body before they could finally escape, must not the masculine condition be sustained in compulsory rebirths?

We find this state of mind flourishing in the south, whose rather nonchalant mentality is diametrically opposed to the basic principles of Buddhism. It was among the Chinese, the Malays, the Thais and the Sinhalese, peoples of a merry, carefree nature, that there spread the Jātakas, those optimistic episodes from the Buddha's previous existences. Here deliverance was reserved for those who adopt the monastic life, and, for the generality of men, a happy future after death was assured for everyone who housed or fed the monks. Plainly then, when the hour of Buddhism's degradation struck, it would be in these lands: the Master would no longer be regarded as a teacher, but as a Liberator come to succour mortals by bearing their burden. There followed a relapse into complete deism, ritual religion and magic.

The northern populations, on the other hand, living a hard life in often harsh regions, appear duly to have seen the Buddha as 'the enlightener', without predestination or divine election or redemption. They held that Deliverance may be won by anyone who wishes it, and that it is only gained by those who follow the teaching. That man alone is free who understands.

But while, in the south, the masses were abandoning Buddhism to the monks, the peoples living northwards of the Ganges threw themselves into a spiritual offensive, invading Buddhism so far as to introduce all the local myths into it, and the magical beliefs which the Buddha had attempted to extirpate. Simplicity turned into undisciplined profusion.

BUDDHIST PSYCHOLOGY

Buddhist psychology—if by this term we mean the science that aims at a knowledge of the mechanisms of the psyche and of the derangements it can undergo—Buddhist psychology is on this point almost non-existent. It is not concerned with ideas either, or with opinions or the history of the development of consciousness. For a Buddhist there can be no knowledge of what we term the *psyche*: for according to the Buddha there only exist fleeting states, whose conjunction can in no way be considered a coherent whole. At the very most one might speak of this philosophy as a dialectical pragmatism with a rationalist basis, whose general tenor we could plausibly regard as psychological.

It is a trend, primarily, that sets problems and does not claim to provide their answers. There is little speculation, in fact, but a practicality whose strength we can appreciate from the 'arrow' parable which follows. The Buddha's only regard is for experiment, verification and proof; yet so debatable does he judge them that he holds it of the first importance to subject the reality of the phenomenon or of the thought to the critical sense.

In the Rules he never fails to stress the uselessness, if not the danger even, of idle questions; and he gives a familiar example in story form.

> A man was struck by a poisoned arrow. Tell me what would have happened if the invalid said, 'I will not have my wound dressed until I know the name of the man who injured me, until I know whether he is a noble or a Brahmin, a Vaiśya or a Śūdra. I will not let myself be tended until I am told to what family he belongs, whether he was tall or short or of middle height, of what wood the bow that shot the arrow that wounded me was made, . . . etc.' The man died of his wound.

And, added the Blessed one, 'Likewise with the doctor who attends him: what matters it who he is or whence he comes provided he can cure?'

53

That personal experience which Buddhist practice aims to produce, results essentially in a transformation of the adept's way of thinking, feeling and acting. In point of fact we are dealing not with a therapy that tends to modify the mental state of a limited number of individuals, so as to integrate them better in a given social order; but rather with one which, on the contrary, applies to *all* human beings. One might almost say that Buddhism considers all mankind aberrant: mankind in its entirety is the patient, and not a few individuals.

Gautama gave prominence to that general kind of malady that consists of a conflicting duality of thought, and he attributed it to a deficiency in our perceptive faculty: in other words, to ignorance or unawareness. This duality is best exemplified by the cleavage of experience into subject and object, i.e. into the person who thinks, or observes, and the thing thought or observed.

In this way, therefore, although the Buddha's initial standpoint had been that of a moralist, circumstances forced it to evolve by degrees into the investigation of a basic psychological question: that of the ego. To strike at the roots of Desire, which causes all our ills, he had to demonstrate its inanity: the answer lay in a dissection of our idea of this ego.

He drew attention first of all to the fact that what we call 'I' is a mere abstraction of memory, and only represents recollections entered in it, giving a misleading impression of continuity. The only valid ego is that of the given instant, concentrated, therefore, into one's immediate experience: the painful duality arises when the individual at this moment tries to bring an, in fact non-existent, 'Me' into play.

For the Buddhist it is of little consequence to look upon release from his suffering as a future objective: all that counts is the identity of one's 'I' with one's present thoughts. It would be a mistake to think that this confinement, and consequent ephemeral nature, of the 'I' rule out any chance of bringing about a general modification in a mind whose outlook is strongly focused on the present moment: quite to the contrary, the renunciation of a false 'I' has a liberating effect, once the thoughts of the moment cease indulging in misinterpretation.

No becoming; but neither is there interest in what is past. The analysis of a causal chain would take us back from the individual to Adam and Eve. One does not rid oneself of an existing wrong perception by discussing the details of its genesis. We are only conditioned by the past on account of our present wrong perception, and Buddhist therapeutics consists precisely in considering the past as no less abstract than the 'I', and in not allowing either of them to invade the concrete experience of the present.

Another and more subtle snare is set to catch our understanding: would it not be tempting to see in the disappearance of the 'I' a regressive surrender of the psyche to primitive impulses of the Unconscious?

Just as breathing, circulation and optical, tactile, muscular or thermic stimuli operate in the body without the intervention of consciousness, but by unconscious processes, so it may be supposed that, in an analogous manner on the psychic plane, we are at certain moments in possession of an important truth, or vehicles for some rare observation.

There, ultimately, is the key. The very corner-stone of the Doctrine, as it has been in effect since the Buddha's time, was rediscovered by the exponents of 'analytical psychology', with such differences, naturally, as arise from the Western and Eastern systems. For us, the individual regarded as ego observes, perceives and checks his experiential world. For the Buddhist, since 'a hand cannot grasp itself', the ego is an abstract and non-effective agent, which cannot perform any action or effect any psychological change. But one therapy has proved its efficacy in both halves of the world, viz. the fusion of the Conscious with the Unconscious. 'The East puts its trust in the Unconscious, whose wisdom it seeks to release in all its profundity' (A. Watts).

The causal nexus: The Buddha held that man was an aggregate of five basic elements (the five *skandhas*, lit. 'heaps'), reacting intimately one upon the other:

Material qualities (*rūpa*),
Sensation (*vedanā*),
Perception (*saṃjñā*),
Co-ordination (the *saṃskāras*), and
Consciousness (*vijñāna*).

None of them of course is stable, any more than are their 'owner' and the various ways in which they can be combined. The number of permutations effected by these skandhas is greatly increased, moreover, when the four elements (earth, air, fire, and water), the principle of intellect, and the idea of space are added to the picture. Meanwhile, each state is the starting-point for a succeeding state: this is *karma*. The linked series which follows gives a synopsis of the process:

(*a*) Desire combined with ignorance determines an act.

(*b*) Performance of the act leaves an impression and gives rise to the consciousness of an 'I'.

(*c*) Impression and ego-consciousness tend to assert one's individual existence.

(*d*) But individual existence can only manifest its reality through the senses.

(*e*) These senses, by severing and connecting, bring contact with the outside world.

(*f*) Now contact begets feeling.

(*g*) There is no feeling without the generation of a craving— the craving to prolong or renew.

(*h*) The craving aims to appropriate the desired object.

(*i*) This appropriation likewise results in a Becoming.

(*j*) All becoming brings about birth (taking this word in its broadest sense, i.e. a new state not precisely similar to the one preceding).

(*k*) And all birth, by the very fact of its occurrence, entails suffering through non-possession and loss, the degradation of old age, and certain death at the end.

> Of things which proceed from a cause
> Their cause the Tathāgata has told,
> And also their cessation;
> Thus teaches the great ascetic.　　(Vinaya-Pitaka.)

This theory of the causal nexus undoubtedly represents the most important part of the Buddhist teaching. It was taken up in various forms by the different schools, who superimposed on it an involved, if not sometimes contradictory, dialectic; and it must correspond fairly closely to the Buddha's own leading idea.

Our being, as we suppose it, has no distinct personal existence. We may liken it to the separate images of a moving picture: each of them proceeds from the previous one and foreshadows the next, yet only the one that is visible, for the shortest imaginable period, in the field of light has any life. Whilst it is granted that phenomena exist in themselves, they are not linked to any 'Substance'; and that strips them of any permanent fixity. The cardinal error—and one fraught with painful consequences—is to believe in an abiding principle.

Speaking to the group of five monks who were his first disciples, the Buddha adds:

> The body, O monks, is not the Self; sensation is not the Self; perception is not the Self; the constructions [predispositions] are not the Self, and neither is consciousness the Self. . . . Perceiving this, O monks, the disciple sets no value upon the body, or upon sensation, or upon the constructions, or upon consciousness. Setting no value upon them, he becomes divested of passion. Through freedom from passion he is emancipated, and in him, emancipated, there arises the knowledge of his emancipation; and then he knows that rebirth is destroyed, that he has lived the holy life, that he has done what was to be done, and that there is no more becoming this or that for him.

These famous words, recorded in the Vinaya-piṭaka, form what is known as the Second Assertion.

The Soul: It follows that the soul—i.e., roughly speaking, the aggregate of feeling, knowledge and volition—is only a stream of states; and we cannot qualify these states by adding the words 'of consciousness', either, for the consciousness of their existence is, more often than not, absent. And even if we had any chance to preceive them, the conscious apprehension of their changes would be overwhelmed by the rapidity with which they succeed one another. Between any two clear glimpses that we might have of these states there would intervene a whole series of others of which our judgement would be falsified by misconstruction.

It seems, however, that the causal continuity is never broken: there is no abrupt innovation or, to use a biological term, mutation. It is this quality of continuity, after all, that allows the practised adept to dam the current and, in his concentration, to follow each state from the time of his birth right up to his transformation into someone else.

This impermanence of the soul does not imply capricious change, any more than the modification continually going on in one's body amounts to a general metamorphosis. Our own science of psychology has in this respect confirmed what the Buddha was trying to teach twenty-five centuries ago.

The distinct, coherent ego does not exist, therefore; there are only egos, each of which, though it goes to make up a particular momentary ego, is not *the* ego. Nor may their combined effect be taken as an 'I': any more than a lake interrupting the flow of a watercourse *is* that river. The Master went farther: he ignored —or even denied—the Self, that is, the existence of the soul as spiritual substance or duration.

> It were better, O disciples, that you took the physical body for the Self than the mind. The body subsists for a moment but that which you call mind is produced and dispersed in perpetual transformation.
>
> Just as a monkey disporting himself in the forest seizes one branch, then abandons it directly to cling onto another, so, O disciples, does that which you call mind, thought, knowledge, take shape and dissolve unceasingly.

This discovery completely ruined the Brahmanical idea of Ātman. There remained only a universe made up of phenomena (*dharma*) and successive states (*saṃskāra*), conspicuous for their transitoriness. This ocean of impermanence is but an ocean of sorrows repeated to infinity.

' Knowledge comes into existence in freedom:
I am freed!' The second affirmation.
(11th century).

This denial of the soul as a 'constant' might be accepted without further discussion if the notion of rebirth did not itself involve a rather thorny problem.

If we refer the matter to Gautama's own teaching, rebirth does not mean reincarnation, the migration of a soul: and since nothing of the being that dies passes into the new one there ought not to be any real relation between the different rebirths. So we cannot identify them with transmigration in the Indian sense—a transmigration of the god into himself. Yet the new being must pay for the old as a result of karmic judgement, which operates with the force of natural law; so that one is driven to suppose that 'something' that has animated one creature (man, animal, deity, or demon) goes on after death to animate another, on a higher or lower level. 'Something' is tossed about in an incessant hithering-and-thithering (*saṃsāra*) of assorted existences, and, since death cannot end matters, floats on the dismal ocean of successive births.

Then what is this 'something' that is reincarnated? In the new creature from which previous karman exacts payment, is it the same 'something' that was bound to a body before? In other words, is the new creature the 'same' one?

On this, as on any metaphysical point, the Buddha did not commit himself, however sharply his disciples raised the question. Deeming the elucidation of the problem unprofitable, he discouraged in advance any attempt to find its solution, indicating that what is reborn is not the same, nor something else either.

This answer is less equivocal than it looks. Suppose that certain peaks of a submerged continent project out of the sea. Then imagine that these peaks are swallowed up and that others belonging to the same adaptable continent emerge from the waters. They will not be the *same* as the previous ones, and yet they will not be *different*.

The Buddhists themselves have wavered somewhat at the prospect of knowledge and continuity without proximate recollection, discrete memory, and transmigrations in which no 'I' is present. One has only to read the *Milinda-pañhā* or Questions of King Menander (a debate from the early period), to catch the essence of this perplexity.

—I am called Nāgasena, O king. But that is only a convenient designation, for there is no Ego here to be found.
—What then is this Nāgasena, your reverence? For truly, if there is no Ego to be found, there no longer exists merit or demerit; no one does, or causes to be done, wrong acts; and there is no fruit of Karma, good or bad. Is the hair of the head Nāgasena? Or the nails, teeth, skin, flesh, sinews, bones, marrow, urine or brain? Is one of these things, or their conjunction, Nāgasena?
—Nay, great king.
—Then, do you mean that there exists something other than the five skandhas?
—By no means, O Lord of men.

And the text adds: 'To every question Nāgasena answered "No".'

Unreality of the phenomenal world: The notion of impermanence had to be supported by that of unreality.

Brahmanical India has always remarked an incompatibility between One, Infinite God, considered as real, and a real world existing outside Him. Its questions about the creation of the cosmic structure have been 'why?', and nothing to do with our 'how?' Whereas for the occidental the world is real—allowing for such adjustments as the mind may make to physical and cosmical appearances that need revision—the Indian accepts what may be supposed beyond the investigation of our senses: he does not refuse to take first causes into consideration under the pretext that being non-perceptible they must be non-scientific.

It was natural then that the Buddha should deem the perceptible a downright infirmity. He did not claim that the world was unreal in itself, but condemned as vain illusion the vision we claim to have of it. In a formal denial that he had ever taught the destruction of whatever reality there may be, he states forcibly: 'There does exist an unborn, not become, not made, uncompounded; and did it not exist, there would be no possible escape for what is born, has become, is made and is compounded.'

Rejecting divine reality in the same way, he succeeded in ridding the mind of all that can divert it from its only valid goal: to be the subject and object of Knowledge.

The only firm ground that is left, therefore, is MĀYĀ, the relativity of things, the illusory world of phenomena, ruled with strict determinism by the law of cause and effect. The Buddha eschewed the sterile examination of first causes as well as belief in the accuracy of sense-perceptions. It was of little concern to him why and how it is that man must exist, why and how he has entered the dread circle of rebirths. He did not puzzle over theories of infinite space and time, or seek to know whether there was a beginning or not, and whether there will be an end. The only thing that matters for mankind is what the Doctrine supplies: the means of escaping from the cycle of rebirths.

Here the law of causality imposed a simple inference. If we do away with the cause of pain, we shall know no pain. Now this cause, as we have seen, is none other than the desire to win gratification, which desire is supported by the ignorance that makes us suppose an illusory world to be true. The first step, therefore, must be to eliminate all consciousness based on the pseudo-experience of the senses. When this is done, and all the elements of the universe are reduced to the value nought, the mind can move without hindrance in a total void.

Truth—a truth so absolute that opposites are harmoniously reconciled in it—is to be found outside ourselves. We cannot expect it until we are utterly emptied of all belief in a phenomenal reality. It then reveals itself to us by means of an Enlightenment.

It is intriguing to follow the sequence of deductions pursued with the strictest rationalism and logic by the Buddha. The sensile world being void of all reality, its reactions upon our senses are therefore equally void; and our ideas, based upon sensory data, are void of truth. It follows that our volitions, the product of these ideas, are in their turn without foundation. The synthesis of these several groups of elements (what we call consciousness) is thus a pure mirage.

The natural conclusion is that there is no such thing as consciousness, and that our 'I' disintegrates when subjected to scrutiny. 'The mind itself is an illusion' ran the teaching, a conclusion which Schopenhauer would certainly have embraced if he had exhausted the implications of his famous dictum, 'The world is my Representation.'

In spite of what may be inferred, the Doctrine thus preached was in no way a materialist one. It refuses to regard the information of the senses, and the use we put this to, as valid data. A synthesis of illusory phenomena being of no greater validity than its elements, the unity Consciousness wishes to avail itself of is false. This is the point at which the notion of consciousness breaks down. It reverts to the rank of the objects of Cognition, whereas the play of illusions had made us think that, by introspection, it could be the *subject* of this Cognition, i.e. the observer. The evidence shows, however, that so long as it remains in the world of phenomena the mind is incapable of filling the two rôles at once, any more than a needle can prick itself, or a knife cut its own blade.

NIRVĀṆA

Few of the Doctrine's terms have occasioned more commentaries, or been the object of as many interpretations, as the state of perfect awareness—Deliverance—in a word, NIRVĀṆA (*nir* 'out', *vā* 'to blow').

The Buddha did not dwell upon the definition of Nirvāṇa, no doubt because he judged it, as he judged many things, not 'profitable'. He simply spoke of *Non-being*, allowing it to be understood that he referred in that way to deliverance from rebirths. To be more specific would be to possess *a priori* knowledge, and hence to attain without effort. But this farthest goal involves a long journey before one comes to its discovery.

It cannot be a question of heaven. Gautama did recognize paradisal abodes, and to that extent had not broken with Indian beliefs, but he taught that their inhabitants—the gods—were only there for a limited stay, being condemned, by virtue of their karma, to the cycle of rebirths like the rest of us.

He himself only became Buddha, only attained Nirvāṇa, that is, beyond which there are no more rebirths, after an interminable series of earthly existences ending in Enlightenment.

The credit for properly stating the problem of Nirvāṇa, in 1876, goes to Eugène Burnouf, who made the tenets of the various schools his starting-point. The subject is authoritatively dealt with by Th. Stcherbatsky in *The Conception of Buddhist Nirvāṇa* (1927).

The first hypothesis is that Nirvāṇa is a final state of rest which man enters when meditation detaches him from the phenomenal world. Here the individual comes into possession of his own strength as it really is, i.e. independently of all that surrounds him. One then has a state of individual life that keeps both its identity and its activity.

A theistic explanation envisages a loftier state. Man, setting aside the outer world and the inner world, succeeds in detaching himself from the phenomena both of his own life and of all relative life. He no longer feels any but Universal existence in him, and cannot distinguish himself from the Cosmos—essential Divinity, or Nature.

Lastly, a third, flatly atheistic conception entails an irreversible disappearance from individual life and from universal life: it is nothingness.

The above, it should be said, are clear-cut hypotheses in which the spirit of Western methodology is discernible. Less inclined to a black-and-white view, the Buddhists who tend to one or other of these suppositions are not so neatly divided between God and annihilation, All and Nothing.

Evidently, since the Buddha's fundamental idea was the negation of all life, we are not required to transfer it into eternity. If the Hīnayāna doctrine—which we shall treat in greater detail further on—sees nothing in Nirvāṇa but an indeterminate cessation of becoming, the Mahāyāna Buddhists who preserve an individual, withdrawn from phenomena, stray from the primitive idea just as much as those who annihilate the individual.

Our thought can only get round the notion of Nirvāṇa if it accepts a cessation of possible transmigrations, beyond its rational mechanism. Then it has to choose between a theist and a nihilist solution. Meanwhile, whatever the purely Buddhist interpretation may be, one comes close to a total negation. As Denis Saurat pertinently remarks, this, for our Western mentality, is the dark side of the human mind. Not indeed that this 'dark side' is absent from Gnosticism, Manichaeism, Catharism, and perhaps even Christianity, but it must be agreed that Buddhism brings the force of this negative principle to its highest point.

Perhaps it is legitimate to suppose that the Buddha refrained from defining Nirvāṇa other than by the neologism *Non-being* precisely because he saw in it a concept indispensable for the mind's entry into contemplation. In this sense, all the notions a Buddhist might have of the 'nirvanic' absolute merely represent different steps necessary for spiritual progress, steps intended to vanish when complete Knowledge is obtained.

Coomaraswamy has defined Nirvāṇa rather well as a *finish*, in the double sense of one's being both ended and perfected. It is neither a place nor an effect; it is not in time; it is not obtained by any kind of means. Yet it 'is', and can in a way be seen. The means employed in practice are not in themselves a way to attain Nirvāṇa but instruments to remove all that disturbs our vision of it: 'Even as a lamp brought into a dark room allows us to distinguish what was there already.'

Delivered for ever from rebirth,
the Buddha enters Nirvāṇa.
(Chinese gilt bronze.)

This theory of an ultimate Non-being existing beyond Divinity was no answer to the desire for a positive God that every human being harboured, and still harbours, within him. Certainly this desire has evolved since man, filled with fears and hopes, first refused to disappear totally after death. The craving for even a relative immortality, often mingled with fear, has quite naturally been allied with a feeling of cosmic unity. And to speak of Unity is to speak of a Unifier too, in creation as in preservation, viz., God.

This picture of the supreme Deity entailed its being the last haven of an 'I' living on after death purged of all earthly pollutions to the point of dissolving in It. The primitive idea of complete or partial after-life was gradually to lose ground to a universal God, at first external and later internal. The Buddha made no attempt to kill the idea of God. He simply did not embody it in his doctrine; and so it stayed alive under the surface of early Buddhism. India did not remain deaf to the echoes of a primeval deism: and so we shall see it adapting the Buddhist notion of Nirvāṇa, shaping the soul, setting problems that call for no solution—in short, deriving religions, often exuberant but always suited to the various Far-Eastern racial stocks, from one of the most severe philosophical doctrines ever taught.

BUDDHIST ETHICS

The Buddha was little given to metaphysical digressions, and left the road clear for interpreters; but his teaching made up for this with practical rules. The individual must be convinced of the general misery of life, of the causes of this misery and of the painful consequences of the illusion with which our senses supply us, but he must also conform to strict rules of life in order to fulfil himself on the spiritual plane. This is how his karma will be lightened, and thus he will perhaps be able to obtain deliverance from further rebirths while in this existence.

Beings, O monks, are responsible for their deeds. Their actions mould them and are their parents, and return upon them. . . .

[In the case of bad karma] there are two possible destinations: either the Niraya hell, painful in the extreme, or the womb of an animal that does not walk straight, a snake, scorpion, millipede, mongoose, cat, mouse, owl, or any other animal that assumes a furtive gait on catching sight of a human being. . . . For those whose discrimination is right, two destinations are possible: either that of heaven, pleasant in the extreme, or to be brought to life in a highly placed family, of Brahmins, of nobles, or of great householders. . . . It is thus that being issues from the resurrection of being, according to past acts. (*Anguttara-Nikāya*.)

Hence the Doctrine, which starts out in this way from a personal ethic, presents itself straight away as a social ethic whose rules will act upon causes with more success than a frontal attack.

Good and Evil: Buddhist morality postulates, in principle, that the individual must cease to differentiate himself from his neighbour. Hence the conceptions of good and evil are personal as much as altruistic. Evil is the satisfaction of a desire; it is wrong done to others. Good, on the other hand, implies a personal sacrifice along with respect for every mind, and likewise for every life, even that of an enemy. Here we have the doctrine of non-violence (*ahimsā*) and the assumption of an inner 'unassailability' as a defence against evil, an attitude extolled two thousand five hundred years later by Mahatma Gandhi. This Buddhist non-violence was subsequently taken over by the Jains as one of their cardinal virtues: if one cannot avoid a snake one must submit to being bitten by it rather than kill it.

The belief in one's own reality, as in that of others, represents the force that opposes the necessary decomposition of the 'I' into its elements: The Buddhist will have no room for egoism any more than for 'individualism'.

Charity will be neither a sentimental act of helping one's neighbour nor, following the Indian conception, an act of devotion to divinity. It marks one step in the stony path of personal detachment. It testifies to an acceptance of brotherhood in

Nature: yet not a Franciscan brotherhood, made of love, but rather a slightly condescending benevolence towards what does not belong to the human species. 'Let no one forget his own duty for the sake of another's, however great; let a man, after he has discerned his own duty, be always attentive to his duty.'

Contempt for the body: The basis of the training, however, is less a morality—as we understand that word—than a demeanour of the body and mind towards oneself and towards other people. In particular it aims at a watchful discipline over the body, with which human beings are only too prone to become infatuated. 'Within this very body, mortal as it is and only six feet in length, I do declare to you are the world and the origin of the world, and the ceasing of the world, and likewise the Path that leads to the cessation thereof.'

Thus it is that, at the time of his development, the future monk must learn to see the 'thirty-two parts' of the body in all their impurity. He will eventually only conceive of our 'nine openings' according to their ability to secrete loathsome substances. He must consider the horrible decomposition which awaits the body and, to this end, he is urged to frequent cemeteries and crematoria. He will acquire such a disgust for what his senses offer him that he will no longer succumb to the insatiate desire to see, touch, breathe, and so on. He will thus be freed from a fallacious servitude:

> Make a parchment of your flayed skin,
> Make a pen of your bones,
> Make ink of your blood,
> And write the teaching of the Master.

Renunciation: The individual, more or less determined by his birth (probably through what we style heredity) and by the education he receives in childhood, has thus a margin of free will. Since the freedom at his disposal depends directly on his freedom of judgement, it is this faculty which must be exercised —allowing of course for the mistakes one may make if one does not determinedly bar the way to illusion. In particular, judge-

Head of an ascetic. (3rd–4th centuries A.D.)

ment of oneself will proceed from a relentless analysis; each feeling, each volition will be dissected into its elements. This 'stripping down' will take away their power, and the mind's freedom will then only have reasonable motives to call into play.

In this way the adept will at last rid himself of the 'ten depravities': desire engendered by the senses, hatred, presumption, blindness, ignorance, opinion, doubt, impudence, negligence, and even simple indiscretion through lack of good judgement.

Certainly he will not reach this point without many times falling back into the mire. But a repentance backed up by firm resolutions and sincere public confession, will allow him, if not to redeem himself, at least to practise no longer the three sins of the body (fornication, theft, and murder), the four sins of speech (frivolous talk, lying, perjury, and slander) and the three sins of the mind (malice, covetousness, and heresy).

On the other hand he will practise the eight Buddhist virtues: love of truth, self-respect, chastity, humility, charitable benevolence, compassion, asceticism, cheerful submission to pain and to all unpleasant experiences.

The renunciation must extend to an indifference to the fruit of one's acts after death. Since there is no continuity of soul, and no Ātman, since it is only a question of breaking the cycle of rebirths, the true Buddhist will not envisage any future happiness resulting from the perfection he acquires: he will deserve Nirvāṇa in order to be more capable of renouncing it. 'Abandon even good, and evil all the more: he who has reached the other shore has no use for rafts.'

Purity: But the repudiation of sin, the repentance of offences committed, the practice of virtues and renunciation serve only to keep a sort of moral account-book of merits or deviations from the rule, each entailing a positive or negative sanction in this life and in rebirths to come. More is needed.

The Sage taught that an action must be considered as good or bad according to the purity or impurity of the state of mind. Thus a given act is consistent with morality not because it is based on precepts or does not infringe prohibitions, but because it flows from a pure state of mind. Purity is defined as freedom from all desire (*lobha*), all hatred (*dvesha*, Pāli *dosa*) and all loss of awareness (or ignorance, *moha*). It is the very essence of the moral code.

Buddhist ethics is severely and strictly personal; it depends neither on the intervention of any—even a perfectly just—deity, nor on a 'submerging' of the individual in this deity. Yet the attitude of a Buddhist shut up in himself in an inexorable mental and spiritual discipline would not entirely satisfy morality. Every subject, in fact, is directly or indirectly bound up with the collective; which implies that individual karma is more or less subordinated to what one might name 'collective karma': in this fashion one comes to acknowledge the illogically hard lot of certain individuals. A genuine Buddhist will not then get lost in justified but vain recriminations: he will accept a painful lot, not apprehending the reasons for it, and will be able to derive a lesson for the future from it.

In practice Buddhist ethics shows itself scarcely different from that which the Brahmins taught. Both require us to banish egoism, dam up sensuality, and indulge in none but noble thoughts, words and deeds; they extol the pre-eminence of the spiritual life over the lower, earthly life; and they value the deed according to the spirit in which it is performed.

There is an expression in the texts that is frequently met with: 'not to be defiled'; this allusion, which relates to the purity of the lotus 'never soaked by the water' above which it opens out its corolla, aims in fact at an absence of defilement of the individual by human affairs. It is not by sin alone that the subject may be polluted, but also by the practice of good. As C. G. Jung has said, virtue is capable of being still more dangerous for man than vice. It is perhaps in this conception of purity that the difference from Brahmanical ethics resides.

Buddhist purity does not lie in the avoidance of a formal pollution: it resides in its entirety in freedom outside certain chains whose weight the Brahmins had not felt, and even in the emancipation from virtue.

THE OLD SCHOOL OF WISDOM

Dating from at least the fifth century B.C., the Buddhism known as the **Old School of Wisdom** was, if not original, still very near to the Buddha's preaching, or so one must suppose. To grasp it properly, we must come back to the Indian mind of that time.

Two aspects were present, which did not indeed clash, but hardly influenced each other deeply either: the man in the street, from the Kshatriya to the Śūdra, and the Brahmin, specialist in relations with the deity.

At all times the climate of India has affected the vigour of its people and limited any revolutionary tendency. The Indian will could not of its own accord shake off the order established by Brahmā, and had allowed itself to be confined in the caste framework. All activity was therefore concerned with the exploration of a well-defined universe, and a universe moreover that did not go beyond a purely Indian Olympus. The terrestrial world was considered relatively unimportant, and, besides, did not exceed the limits of the peninsula—no doubt on account of a geography which isolated it from its neighbours with barriers of mountain and sea.

For his part the Brahmin had reserved the practice of

sacrifice. Paul Mus has defined the meaning of the Brahmanical sacrifice perfectly: an operation intended to cause the sacrificer, himself a particle of an original Divinity dispersed in all creatures (Prajāpati), to mount up to heaven with the flame. By the gestures with which he disposed the goblets of the *Soma*, liquor of immortality, by his formulae and chanting, and above all by devoting his mind to the meaning and importance of the sacrificial act, the Brahmin—or, by proxy, whoever he was officiating for—returned to the original source, became the Divinity.

Amongst the Kshatriya, Vaiśya, or Śūdra castes as with the Brahmins, there existed no personality capable of shaking off, with love or hatred, a present which was only a petrified past. The strength and at the same time this as it were living death of India lay in a collective spirit rejecting the idea of any future in which to put one's hope and heedless too of any recollection of the past. It must be observed moreover that the collective spirit characterized the antiquity of all lands. In Egypt, in Israel, in Mesopotamia, the individual never counted—except of course the king, although he was only the supreme incarnation, religious and not temporal, of the collectivity.

The Indian yogins themselves could not be regarded as individually active. Cut off materially and socially from the collective by their own will, they belonged to it spiritually. Dreaming solely of what is beyond time and space, going off in their meditation to conquer everlasting heavenly kingdoms, they utilized their thought to function as a sixth sense capable of 'seeing' the void.

But neither Brahmins, nor yogins, nor the other castes had paid any attention to the sufferings entailed in the mere fact of existence. Or if they had noted it, they accepted it as fate. Death, with the soul's departure to the moon and its return from there to earth in the midst of the rain, was only an episode. One could only escape from rebirth in certain optimum sacrificial conditions which would allow the soul to cross through the 'narrow doorway of the sun' and to know an ocean of felicity whence there was no return. But even this happy conclusion did not have the purpose of removing the soul from the pain of existence.

Śāriputra: Primitive Buddhism, in its discovery of suffering, set the gods aside and saw only temporary incarnations in their persons. The worship paid to celestial powers had then no more reason to exist than the mediating priest.

There remained nevertheless the propensity to which the Indian mind had always been attached: to know more. But Buddhist knowledge had to be brought to bear no longer on the origin of worlds and the organization of the universe but upon man; and this conception reached far beyond Indian man. Also, the setting aside of gods and Brahmins was to have, to all intents and purposes, the material accompaniment of the neglect of castes. The individual had made his appearance.

If Gautama appeared as the overall revolutionary thinker, the organizer of the Doctrine's practical dissemination was his disciple ŚĀRIPUTRA, 'son of Śāri'.

This Indian from the kingdom of Magadha, born in a family of Brahmins, entered the religious life at an early age under the guidance of SAÑJAYA, one of those sceptical ascetics whom one might compare with the Greek Cynics. After hearing the Buddha, he left all to follow him, and was not long in receiving Enlightenment in his turn.

A realist by nature, he set about assisting the Master by taking charge of the teaching. Displaying a pre-eminently analytical intellect, he organized the material in such a way that everyone could study, understand, and remember it with ease.

Tremendously erudite, thanks to his birth, he had acquired true wisdom from his master. He excelled all the other disciples and played an immeasurably more important part in the diffusion of the Doctrine than ĀNANDA, the Blessed one's favourite pupil. For the Sthavira-vādins (Pali *Theravādin*) and Sarvāstivadins of later times he represents a kind of second founder.

Thus the Buddhism of the earlier centuries may with justification be called the SCHOOL OF ŚĀRIPUTRA or OLD SCHOOL OF WISDOM. This Wisdom was praised by Śāriputra as the highest of the Five Cardinal Virtues (wisdom, faith, vigour, mindfulness, and concentration). For this master, only the practice of Wisdom could ensure final salvation.

The arhats: It is now that we meet with a new concept, that of the ideal man, the complete sage, the saint who has reached the topmost point of spiritual development—in short the *arhat*. From the time of the Buddha and Śāriputra this term was applied to ascetics. Only subsequently was it restricted to wholly freed, perfect saints.

The derivation of the word *arhat* is held by some present-day Buddhists to come from *ari* (enemy) and *han* (to slay): the arhat would thus be he who destroys his passions. Relying on recent semantic data, Conze refers it rather to the root *arh* (to be worthy of), of which it is the present participle.

The arhat (Chinese *lo-han* or *a-lo-han*) wins salvation by means of a meditation resulting, through trance, in eight successive stages of mystical ecstasy. He draws away from the material world by abandoning one after another desire, thought, joy, and spiritual well-being. Then freeing himself from the immaterial world, he will know the four infinities—of space, consciousness, the region where nothing exists, and lastly the region where there is no longer perception or even absence of perception. Each of these states is only a stage: 'It is not enough,' taught the Buddha. 'Abandon it and go beyond.' When these eight stages are passed, and all perception ended, it is Nirvāṇa.

This image of the arhat makes him comparable to a kind of hero, confronting and breaking down the obstacles on the path to Deliverance. No better portrait of him can be given than by quoting the following passage taken from the Avadāna-śataka, the Sanskrit collection of stories, attributed to the Buddha, to show the consequences of karma.

> He exerted himself, he strove and struggled, and thus he realized that this circle of 'Birth-and-Death', with its 'Five Constituents' is in constant flux. He rejected all the conditions of existence which are brought about by a compound of conditions, since it is their nature to decay and crumble away, to change and to be destroyed. He abandoned all the 'defilements' and won Arhatship. On becoming an Arhat, he lost all his attachment to the 'Triple World' [i.e. the world of sense desire, the world of form, the formless world]. Gold and a clod of earth

were the same to him. The sky and the palm of his hand were to him the same. He remained cool [in danger] like the fragrant sandalwood to the axe which cuts it down.' (Tr. Conze.)

This militant and piously egoistic aspect of an arhat, conceived amongst the monks of the central Deccan, was replaced in the north by a figure full of compassion, entirely selfless. There, arhatship could lead (though not necessarily) to the state of a *bodhisattva* or archangel. The saint who is freed can accordingly return to save the world: this was the case with the Buddha, whose innumerable previous lives are related in the Jātaka stories. For this work of salvation the bodhisattva used six means: charity, good conduct, energy, meditation, theoretical wisdom, and practical wisdom.

There is, however, a very long road to travel between the beginnings of a state of sainthood and any deliverance granting the power to save the world.

Trance: Apart from the practice of a strong moral discipline and of wisdom, one who is set on becoming an arhat must be able to pass into mystic regions by means of trance.

The word *trance* here means *concentration*. It is the equivalent of the Sanskrit term *samādhi* (which corresponds in structure to the Greek word *synthesis*). In concentration the ascetic narrows his field of attention in a manner and for a time determined by his will. In this way he arrives at a peace without latent tension.

This concentration is obtained in practice through eight degrees of meditation (*dhyāna*), through the 'Four Immeasurables' (*apramāṇa*) and the acquisition of occult powers. The Dhyānas were to become the basis of Yogācāra Buddhism, the Immeasurables that of the Mahāyāna school, and the secret powers that of Lamaism.

The object of the meditations or *dhyānas* is to transcend sensory impressions. To this end, one fixes one's attention on a material object—a lotus flower, an image of the Buddha, a circle drawn with red sand, etc. Having succeeded in suspending all foreign and hence 'unwholesome' thoughts, one must learn to direct one's thoughts on to the selected object. Next it will be possible to go beyond the thoughts which flowed towards and around the object. In the third and fourth dhyānas all consciousness of comfort and discomfort ceases.

The subsequent meditations take one beyond the object: they are 'formless' and apprehend boundless space, limitless consciousness, the void (*emptiness*), ending in a state where there is neither further perception nor non-perception. In this state of near-coma one touches Nirvāṇa 'with one's body'. There is no longer motion, or speech, or thought or, perhaps, unconscious impulse. The 'Self' is in suspension during the whole period of the meditation. Only warmth and the beating of his heart indicate that the ascetic is still alive. This state, however, does not give immediate access to Nirvāṇa: the individual Self must be wholly and finally obliterated in the midst of an infinite Wisdom.

The emotional method of the Immeasurable is more down-to-earth, but can only bear fruit after the practice of at least the third dhyāna. Through friendship towards others, compassion, sympathetic joy, and impartiality (the four Immeasurables) one is set free from all personal preferences and antipathies. One's compassion should have a general character with reference to other people's sufferings, and one's joy should be a concentration on their happiness.

As for the occult powers, they may have corresponded at the start to the psychic forces inevitably called forth by the expectation of a lofty spiritual life, but they were not slow to degenerate. The Doctrine spread among populations much given to magic; and it was bound socially to compromise with practices which it should really have condemned for the dangers they presented —distortion of spiritual aims, exaltation of the Ego, conceit, the search for prolongation of one's 'own' existence.

The Doctrine of Wisdom (*Pra-jñā*), or methodical contemplation of the Doctrine of phenomena, represents the highest Buddhist conception. It evidently took shape in the first centuries after the Buddha's death before being described in the seven volumes of the additional Doctrine (*Abhi-dharma*). As the philosopher Buddhaghosa points out, 'It penetrates into phenomena as they are and destroys their illusion by dispersing the darkness.' *Not to think 'I am such-and-such': this is freedom (Udāna).*

Age-old habit has led us to identify ourselves with objects to such an extent that what happens to them is easily regarded as happening to ourselves, the words 'me', 'mine', and 'I' being used for the explanation we give ourselves of our experiences. To say 'My cup is broken' or 'I have split my nail' is to construct a fictitious self placed above and beyond the five *skandhas*

Prajñāpāramitā, the faculty of transcendent wisdom.
(Java, 14th century.)

of which we have already spoken (see pp. 55–6): matter, feeling perception, volition, and consciousness.

The Doctrine replaces the personal expressions by impersonal ones: the toenail or fingernail is matter, its being split causes an unpleasant feeling, there is perception of trouble and then a reaction to avoid physical discomfort; lastly there is consciousness of all this. Even if an imagined 'I' is a part of the actual experience, the Self is not concerned in it.

Wisdom therefore consists in ceasing to identify ourselves with spurious appurtenances that are not really ours. 'If thoughts or activities come, they do not arise at all out of the mind, but they come from outside and cross the mind as a flight of birds crosses the sky on a windless day' (Sri Aurobindo).

It is not enough to renounce the world of conditioned things by the abandonment of all possessions and by meditation, nor to understand by the practice of trance that the objects of the 'common sense' world are illusory: Wisdom must also attempt to enter into the Unconditioned, i.e. the Absolute.

There we touch on the central point of Buddhism, a point rich in paradox. In the first place, *what* is to enter it?—since the Self must vanish at the very moment it comes into contact with the Unconditioned. Further, nothing can be said or imagined about the Absolute, since it is unrelated to anything: and yet this 'Supreme' Unconditioned absorbs the Conditioned, so that it is at the same time transcendent and immanent—or neither one nor the other. As Conze points out, the only proper answer to these and similar questions about the Absolute is a negative-affirmative, a kind of 'Nyes'. The Absolute itself, undetermined and indeterminable as it is, is merely a provisional conception of the meditator (we dare not say 'of his mind') and must undoubtedly be obliterated with the total extinction of the Self.

THE NEW SCHOOL OF WISDOM

THE EVOLUTION OF BUDDHISM

THE influence of Buddhism was long confined to an elite of Kshatriyas and Brahmins capable of following its arduous teaching.

An order of monks—to which we shall revert—had been created, uniting those who longed to break the chain of rebirths, the more learned among them attempting to elucidate the points on which the Buddha had not given an opinion. The Master had modestly owned that 'what he taught was as abundant as the leaves of a tree, but the truths that had been revealed to him without his teaching them were more numerous than the leaves of the whole forest.' Perhaps he had been hindered by the use of the Prākṛt language, ill-appointed for expressing the transcendental, or perhaps he judged his revelation beyond the grasp of formal thought. The fact remains that the questions left open—particularly the object of Knowledge—gave full scope to interpretative study of all kinds.

The layman contented himself with following the sermons, living under the guidance of the monks, taking part in pilgrimages, and adoring relics contained in stupas. No worship or ceremony, in spite of a latent inclination to magic and to the ancient reverence paid by the people to their gods. The limit to possible irregularities lay in the triple recitation each day of the **formula of the three jewels** (*Triratna*) in which one's loyalty to the Master, the Doctrine, and the Community was affirmed.

> I go to the Buddha as refuge.
> I go to the Dharma as refuge.
> I go to the Saṃgha as refuge.

The Buddhism of Faith: After the Buddha's death, Buddhism had to evolve conceptions more susceptible of being understood and felt. The metaphysical notion of the Ādibuddha,

79

stripped of any historical character, represented but an abstraction of the Absolute only perceptible during mystic ecstasy, and too cold to inspire fervour in a single faith. The bodhisattvas themselves were speculative and without perceptible reality. Self-surrender, renunciation, and fervent devotion must find a support: the initiatory master, the *guru* as the Indians call him. Buddhism was obliged by force of circumstances to take up these antique human attitudes.

Bhakti: The man in the street—the layman—being notoriously incapable of practising a wisdom deprived of any external support, had to fall back on faith. In the Old School this came eventually to rank with wisdom as a virtue. Soon it became 'the easy path' open to all, as opposed to a way of salvation by works or Knowledge.

BHAKTI, the idea of an impassioned love that gives all, asks nothing, and absorbs the whole being in a rapture from which the mind remains absent, makes its appearance in Buddhist doctrine around 400 B.C., but had certainly long struck root in Indian soil. At the same time as it was influencing the Buddha's devotees it inspired a Brahmin worshipper of Kṛshṇa-Vishṇu; the BLESSED LORD'S SONG (Bhagavad-gītā), composed in the third century and inserted in the famous epic of the Mahā-Bhārata, is one of the most magnificent cries of love for the divine that have ever been uttered.

It is perhaps to Ānanda, the disciple who *loved* the Master as a real person, that we must attribute the germ of devotional Buddhism. Unable to resign himself to the loss of his guide, he conceived the idea that entering Nirvāṇa the Buddha had gained the highest stage of the Tushita heaven whence he had descended to save mankind.

If the orthodox doctrine forbade the bearing of such love for the Sage, the faithful were nevertheless very ready to wish that 'the Lord Buddha' had not really died and remained present, although invisible.

Once launched, Bhakti was bound to replace, for the common man, every other practice. We shall see it blossom in the

Mahāyāna school where a fervid devotion is shown to bodhisatt-vas and to the Buddha himself. Lulled by the human love ascending to them, they respond by exalting the worshipper's virtues, help him to rid himself of illusion, anger, hatred, and greed, and protect him against baleful spirits and bad men who have no spiritual ideal. They go as far as granting wishes; avert accidents, shipwrecks and illness; and they can even arrest the fall of the executioner's sword on a condemned man's neck. Thanks to them, women will have the son they desire, caravans cross deserts without being plundered, fires be put out, the cobra's venom lose its power, wild beasts flee, and enemy swords break in the scabbard. What can a Power not do, moved by the adoring devotion of man?

For the layman it was a far cry from the extinction of the Self, from the eight degrees of mystical trance, from emptiness and from impermanence. As a result of a popular humanization of Buddhism, pain, the causes of pain and the means of breaking the painful chain of rebirths were no longer taken into account. In the Buddhism of faith, it was only a question of obtaining the best rebirth, that in the paradise of the Blessed, after one's death.

The requirements were confined to the observation of five rules:

1. To lead a pure life in thoughts, words, and deeds, with a burning desire to become like the Perfect one;

2. To pay inward and outward homage to the Buddha and the bodhisattvas—gifts, and adoration of their transcendent virtues;

3. To invoke the Blessed one by repeating his name: the name, charged with power, makes it possible to acquire the highest virtues. Later on, invocation becomes indispensable, and we have for instance the Sanskrit *Om Namo Amitābhāya Buddhāya* ('obeisance to the Buddha Amitābha!'), in China *Na-mo O-mi-to-fo*, and in Japan *Namo Amida Butsu*;

4. To collaborate with the Buddha, the saviour of the world, in the infinite compassion he displays for all creatures;

5. To meditate upon the perfection and beauty of the bodh-isattvas and the Buddha and to concentrate one's senses until one has visual, auditory, tactile, and olfactory impressions thereof.

The new schools: As the centuries go by, we witness at first not exactly a decline of the Law but a modification rather. The Doctrine itself in this was subordinated to the impermanence of all things. Various methods were proposed to attain the end that the Buddha formulated. The Sage's immediate disciples had already envisaged different paths to salvation: for Śāriputra it was wisdom, for Ānanda gentleness, faith, and fervent adoration, for Maudgalyāyana magical powers.

Obviously the geographical dispersal of the Doctrine has subjected it to the influences of climate, of the hardness or ease of living conditions, and of the mentality of the populations it moved among. The date of introduction and the local beliefs alike played an important rôle in these alterations. Preached in the kingdom of Magadha and spreading at first towards the west and south of India, the Law could not fail to be influenced by the spirit which predominated in the north and east. Interpretations were set against one another, dissension flared up, rivalries, at times very serious, asserted themselves. One century after the Buddha's entry into Nirvāṇa, the devotees of the Old and the New were already opposed. By the end of the reign of king Aśoka (c. 200 B.C.), irreconcilable sects had been formed.

A long-lived conservative element was represented by the Sthaviravādins, who were unwilling to depart from Śāriputra's Old School of Wisdom. They formed the most solid obstacle in the way of the *Great-Assemblists* of the MAHĀSAṄGHIKA school founded by the monk Mahādeva.

This Great Assembly (*Mahā-saṅgha*) included 'monks of lesser attainments' and householders. While the Mahāsaṅghikas condemned the Assembly of the Arhats and their moral and intellectual deficiency—agreeing in this with the Old school—their members showed such a defiant liberalism that their activity never influenced the common people. Although their literature seems to have been fairly abundant, few books remain to allow us to form an opinion of this movement. The most notable trace it has left lies in the impulse given to the formation of a new school, the *Mahāyāna*.

The Emperor Aśoka: 'Two hundred and fifty-six years after the death of the Buddha,' we learn from the Tibetan Li-yul lo-rgyus, 'a king of India named Dharma-Aśoka, having slaughtered a great number of creatures, was restored to virtue by a holy arhat named Ja-śo. Abhorring his old faults, he confessed them.'

ASOKA ('sorrowless') PRIYADARŚIN ('kindly-looking') was none other than the grandson of Candra-gupta, founder of the Maurya dynasty. When he came to the throne in 273, his house reigned over three-fourths of the peninsula, having forcibly put a stop to the rivalries of innumerable warring principalities and republics.

Although the famous Greek Ptolemy Philadelphus, arriving in Patna from Egypt, says of this king that 'he possessed the art of saying one thing and thinking another', it is likely that Aśoka was sincere in his desire to salve his conscience for the frightful massacres that had accompanied his victory at Kaliṅga, on the Coromandel coast. Donning the yellow robe to go and meditate under the sacred fig-tree at Bodh-gayā, he returned after following the novices' rule and performing the compulsory hundred and fifty-six days' pilgrimage. From this moment Buddhism emerges from legend to enter history. For the first time we can refer to texts and to dates carved on stone. Henceforth the stelae erected by this king will be our guide.

One may accuse the sovereign of having too deliberately omitted to cite the Buddha's name; there is no hint of dogma or even mention of Nirvāṇa; yet Aśoka relied on the Buddhist Rule. He condemns popular rites and 'other nursery customs', but is too subtle a politician to attack a tested social convention; so he will in no way meddle with the castes and with the seven classes of Indian society.

The emperor set himself outside all sects, respecting them and letting them be freely honoured, and sought to save human beings. Throwing open his treasury, he sent missionaries to found hospitals and schools, build monasteries, raise stūpas, set up pious columns, and instigate edifying discourses. The smallest township owned a monastery, a hospice, and a caravan-serai to welcome travellers. The roads were shaded with trees to shelter the pilgrims and infirmaries set up for the care of sick animals.

Monks were sent outside India, even as far as Asia Minor. Denis Saurat states that the Buddha was known to the early Christians of Syria; his life reached Europe through several intermediary versions, and was judged so edifying that he was canonized in the sixteenth century as St. Josaphat (Arabic *Judasaf*, Pehlevī *Budasaf*, Bodhisattva).

It has even been claimed that Buddhist monks came to Gaul and Britain.

Aśoka's generosity was bound nevertheless to defeat its own object. Many adepts had joined the Community because of the easy life it offered them. No longer depending on the villagers for their livelihood, the monks lost touch with the secular world. Not until the Mahāyāna had reached its full vigour would the primitive simplicity be regained.

The Councils: Fearing that the eagerness for marvels which reigns in India would render the holy teachings unrecognizable within a century, Aśoka decided to call a council. It was concerned less with dogmas than with codifying the monastic rule once for all.

A First Council had been held at Rājagṛha in 473, the same year as the Buddha's entry into Nirvāṇa. It marks the appearance of the beginnings of the TRIPLE BASKET (Tripiṭaka) comprising:

1. The SŪTRAS or direct teachings of the Buddha written out by Ānanda (see below).

2. The VINAYA, the monastic discipline, instilled by Upāli.

3. The ABHIDHARMA or book of metaphysics. The *Mātṛkā* or original text without commentaries was recited by Kāśyapa.

A Second council was held a century later at Vaiśālī, which completed the work of the first by attempting to reconcile differences and solve material problems facing the Community.

The council over which Aśoka presided in 253 in his capital at Pāṭaliputra did not seek to fix the doctrine, and, in conformity with the Buddha's refusal to name a successor, did not put forward any *spiritual head* of the Buddhist community. Its major pre-occupation was to favour the diffusion of Buddhism by giving it enough material and spiritual strength to resist corruption.

As a matter of fact, the southern Buddhists (the Hīnayānists of Ceylon, Siam, Cambodia, Laos, and Burma) recognize the decisions of this council as most in accordance with the original Buddhism. The Mahāyānists of the north, on the other hand, pass over the council of Aśoka in silence and only apply the term Third to the council held at Jālandhara, in Kashmir.

The canon revised at this assembly was drawn up in Pāli.

The holy scriptures: No incontestable document dating from the time of the Buddha allows us to establish the canon in its primitive form. Such a canon must have existed, for Aśoka, in the rock-inscription at Baihut, mentions what the monks, nuns and lay folk must know, recite and do. The teaching must have remained purely oral until the second century, although texts had probably been written in the language of Magadha.

The writings of the Mahāyānists in Sanskrit having for the most part disappeared and their Chinese and Tibetan translations remaining debatable—and debated—we can best gain a sound acquaintance with Buddhism (that at least of the first centuries of our era) in the Sinhalese Triple Basket.

The texts, as we said, had until then been learnt by heart. Aśoka's son (or younger brother) Mahendra came to Ceylon to found a monastery and recited them. In the first century B.C. the Sinhalese monks wrote them down in Pāli, a language of learning which, like the older Sanskrit, was widely separated from popular speech. It must have been a lengthy task, judging by the number of works, each of which had been repeatedly worked over before reaching its definitive form. Nevertheless it is likely that the broad principles formulated by the Buddha were not perceptibly altered over the years. The SŪTRAS in particular were little tampered with; Ānanda, who reports these words of the Master, always begins his account with 'Thus have I heard. On a certain occasion the Blessed One was dwelling

In the southern countries, the scriptures are written in Pali on dried palm leaves.

at . . .'. But the Buddhist world is still divided over the authenticity of a considerable proportion of the sūtras.

The Hīnayāna Triple Basket: Monastic discipline (VINAYA) makes up the first part of the Tripiṭaka: the governance of the monks guarantees in fact a pure and lasting form of Buddhism. And in the Vinaya the BOOK OF PRECEPTS (*Pātimokkha*, Skt. Prātimoksha) ranks first: it lists the 227 commandments to be obeyed, commandments probably established by the first disciples of Gautama. At every new moon, and at every full moon, the monks must publicly confess their shortcomings and repent before receiving absolution.

Twenty of the Vinaya's treatises (the *kandalas*) set forth in detail the rules of admission, of life, of attention, of exclusion as well as ordinances relating to the nuns.

The second Basket, the *sutta* (Skt. sūtra) or *'main threads'*, deals with canon and religious questions of a general order. This BASKET OF DISCOURSE is composed of five long collections (or *nikāyas*) of dialogues in which the Buddha himself appears, and of explanations of psychology and ethics. There is an enumeration of things reckoned in ones, twos, threes (e.g. the Three Jewels) and so on up to the thirty-four elements of the human organism and the thirty-three points of sainthood.

The Suttapiṭaka also includes the Dhammapada or VERSES ON DHARMA, the *Udāna* or SOLEMN UTTERANCES and the *Theragāthā* or SONGS OF THE ELDERS. The well-known *Jātaka* (BIRTH STORIES) tells of five hundred and fifty of Gautama's past existences and the edifying miracle that distinguishes each one. They represent an invaluable document as regards archetypes, myths of the past, and popular beliefs and legends.

The third Basket (The *Abhidhamma* or FURTHER DOCTRINE) largely written down under Aśoka, deals with ethics and philosophy as well as the refutation of heresies.

The Triple Basket grew considerably up to the fifth century A.D., each doctor making a point of adding his interpretations and writing new treatises (the *śāstras*). One of the most fertile was the philosopher BUDDHAGHOSA (said to have converted Burma) who, about 450, composed the PATH OF PURITY (*Visuddhi-Magga*) for the Sinhalese monastery of Ganthakara.

In addition to these canonical works we should mention the QUESTIONS OF MILINDA (*Milinda-pañha*) in which the great Indo-Greek king Menander debates with the sage Nāgasena.

THE COMMUNITY

Lay Buddhism: If Buddhism has come to be regarded as a religion it still differs from all the others in that it entails no rite, no sacrament, and no formula conferring the right to be a Buddhist. The layman is a Buddhist solely by virtue of accepting the Buddha's teaching as truthful, of conforming to the moral prescriptions, and of contributing to the material support of the community of monks.

He will not reach salvation in this life, for he does nothing to free himself from desire, the cause of suffering: he confines himself to laying up a good incarnation for himself. The principal work of merit consists in the maintenance of the bonzes

and attendance at public preachings. The cult proper amounts to no more than the oblation of flowers, candles and incense in front of statues of the Sage or some image evoking him, such as the imprint of his foot, and to the participation in a few festivals.

The rules taught to the faithful by the monks dwell at length on relations between human beings. Always preceded by the admonition that

> Anger must be overcome by the absence of anger;
> Evil must be overcome by good;
> Greed must be overcome by liberality;
> Lies must be overcome by truth.
>
> (*Dhammapada.*)

the sermon specifies the duties to be performed.

1. Those who have children must keep them from evil, bring them up in righteousness, have them taught, get them married, and leave them an inheritance.

2. For their part, children should support those who have supported them, fulfil the duties demanded of them by the family and preserve its goods, render themselves worthy of their inheritance, and honour their parents' memory after death.

3. The master should show his pupil affection, teach him the worship of goodness and nobility, control his attention; he should not bully or abuse him but on the contrary should praise him to his companions; he should warn him of danger and try to avert it.

4. The pupil should honour his master by rising respectfully before him, serving and obeying him, providing for his wants and listening attentively to his lessons.

5. The husband must love his wife, treat her with consideration and affection, be faithful to her, take care that she is respected and honoured, and offer her the clothes and jewels she needs.

6. As for the wife, she should show her tenderness for her husband, prove chaste, keep the household in order, extend hospitality to her husband's friends and relations and show 'dexterity and zeal in all she has to do'.

7. Between friends, the rule is to give presents, speak kind words to one another, take care of mutual interests, live on an equal footing, and share the gains equitably in any common undertaking. The only good friend is one who watches over others when they are off their guard, protects their property if they are rash, offers them a refuge in case of danger, stays faithful to them in hard times and extends his friendship to their family.

8. Finally, the master should take care of the well-being of his servants; only give them tasks proportionate to their strength; pay and feed them without niggardliness, look after them if they are ill, assure them of a suitable burial, 'share dainties' with them, and grant them a day's leave from time to time.

9. Servants on the other hand should get up before their master, go to bed after him, be content with what they receive if it is just, work cheerfully, defend him, and only address him with deference. They should not abandon him in sickness, sorrow and distress.

Of course, laymen and monks must observe reciprocal duties.

Thus it is that the honest man assists the monk as soon as he apprehends the need, ensures his sustenance, and treats him with respect in words, thoughts, and deeds. The monk in return must dissuade him from vice, exhort him to virtue, bear him the same friendship and compassion he would bear to himself, give him instruction if asked, resolve his doubts and spiritual problems, and smooth his path to Beatitude.

By acting thus, O believers, you will make sure of peace and security in the six points of space. He who honours these six points will be entitled to consideration. Generosity, patience, friendly courtesy, unselfishness, and purity, these are the virtues that are as necessary to Society as a wheel is to a chariot.

In conclusion, it is fitting to recall the observation of Sylvain Levy: 'We witness the spectacle, as contradictory as life and in harmony with it, of a religion founded upon nothingness that carries practical virtues to their utmost pitch.'

Monastic Buddhism: The monk, though ordained, has no priestly functions. But, being more advanced on the path of salvation, he serves as a model for the laity whilst working out his own deliverance. The ritual forms met with in the so-called 'Lamaist' Buddhism—hierarchy, daily psalmody, use of sacred vestments, practice of confession, and use of the rosary—are mere borrowings.

An attitude to the monk more in agreement with the original is found in the Hīnayāna. In Ceylon, or Cambodia, the bonze is not a priest, does not serve as intermediary between man and a deity, and offers no sacrifice. He only represents a brotherhood of men who have left the world. Some, moreover, only take the yellow robe for a time, short or long; for eternal vows do not exist. There are few Nepalese, Burmese, Laotians, or Cambodians, who have not spent some months in a *vihāra* either as novices or, when of age, as monks.

During his last life on earth, the Buddha seems to have been strongly attached to the organization of monastic life, both in the laying down of rules and in the orientation of thought.

He classified thoughts and actions as beneficent (*kuśala*) and helping to lighten the heavy burden of human suffering, as harmful (*akuśala*), or else as indifferent. The training consists of systematically weakening the grip of things which hold back the individual on the way to immortality which he has lost simply by being reborn; it thus aims at verifying mental processes by meditating on them. In this sense, Buddhist thought proves pragmatic and dialectical, rather prone to contradiction and to paradox.

A complete freedom of adherence is offered the monk, for he does not have to concern himself with dogmas. It is as a free agent that he follows the advice on behaviour, thinks and acts. His actions and the expression of his thought hence exactly correspond with his inner attitude of detachment, conviction, ardent aspiration. Thought itself is only a strictly personal instrument, aloof from all proselytism: its justification lies in the results obtained by the monk in his journey to salvation.

The Buddha had condemned mortification practised as such:

having himself experienced its inefficacy, he never regarded it as more than a means to be adopted temporarily if at all. 'There are two things, O disciples, which must be avoided: a life of pleasures, for that is degrading and vain; and a life of mortifications, for that is useless and vain.' The yogin's self-control is not an end but a stage to be passed. Beyond is the Doctrine, valid for all humanity.

At the start all the monks were wanderers going to spread the good word. The first communities were instituted by the Blessed one himself, on lands given by monarchs converted to the Law. Such was the Bamboo Grove at Kośala presented by the king of Magadha. As the Dharma conceived of no distinction between men, no caste separation interfered with admission into the Community: the Brahmin and the pariah went side by side in the observance of the Rule.

To a Brahmin who asked him what was his caste, the Lord replied:

> I am not a Brahmin or rājā's son,
> Nor am I a merchant;
> Nor am I any one at all;
> I fare in the world, a sage, with nothing.
> Wearing a monk's robe, homeless, I go,
> My head shaven and my soul serene,
> Without taint of human concerns;
> It is inept to ask me about my caste.

Coomaraswamy stresses that it would be a mistake to think that the Buddha 'attacked' the caste system: in reality he distinguished the person who is only a Brahmin by his birth from one who is a true Brahmin by his Knowledge, and recalled that the religious vocation is open to men of all stations.

The three monastic Rules: Along with very minute directions such as to sleep on one's right side, to wash one's robe and sash, to live in a dwelling outside the city (at first these were caves), not to eat gluttonously or with one's fingers, not to speak with one's mouth full and to refrain from 'coveting one's neighbour's bowl', the Buddha set up three fundamental rules.

> *'I fare in the world, a sage, with nothing, wearing a monk's robe, my head shaven and my soul serene.'*

First of all, the monk has no right to any property save his nine ritual objects (three articles of clothing, a razor, needles, a filter, a fan, his sash, and his wooden bowl called *pātra*, Pāli *patta*). He must gain his living from alms. Two hours after sunrise he leaves, holding out his bowl for the devotees to put into it the food prepared that morning, using a long ladle to avoid any unseemly proximity. The sole meal of the day should be taken between 9 and 10 o'clock. All food is forbidden after noon, drink alone being permitted.

The alms-bowl is a symbol of sovereignty, and a master has been known to bequeath his to a disciple to mark the handing on of his authority. On receiving the alms, for which he has not begged in words, the monk expresses no thanks. Far from feeling a sense of inferiority, he considers that he has given the believer a chance to increase his merits and practise an important virtue. Mendicancy is a school of discipline; it lowers the neophyte's pride and allows him to live without even the necessities of life.

Secondly, the monk must abhor violence. There was a reaction, about 500 B.C., to sacrifice and a habitual brutality of

The begging bowl is one of the nine objects which the monk may possess. (Found in central Asia, stucco.)

behaviour, not only to men but to animals. The kinship of all creatures, an offshoot of the theory of reincarnation, was allied with the compassion which every human must feel for other beings as much as for himself. In the Udāna, the Buddha does not veil his warnings:

> My thought has wandered in all directions throughout the world. I have never yet met with anything that was dearer to anyone than his own self. Since to others, to each one for himself, the self is dear, therefore let him who desires his own advantage not harm another.

In actual fact, Buddhism did mollify the warlike character of the Mongols and the Tibetans: from the peaceful bearing of the Soyots and Khalkhas of the present day, one can scarcely imagine that these are genuine descendants of the fierce horsemen of Genghis Khan.

The monk, therefore, must abstain from meat, from all that has been killed to feed him. Certain strict sects go as far as to proscribe milk and eggs, obtained by means of an act of procreation. In the south of India, however, fish is permitted, since it is held that it ran itself on to the hook through gluttony.

Finally, celibacy is indispensable, because any relation with a woman may involve an attachment to her and to the child that may be born. The Buddha saw the company of woman as a bond incompatible with the monastic life: one's psychic energy would not remain entirely available for meditation. In any case, he had no great esteem for the feminine character:

> Assuredly one must beware of women. For one who is wise there are more than a thousand foolish or wicked ones. Woman is more secret than the path the fish follows in the water. She is as fierce, and as cunning, as a brigand. She rarely speaks the truth: for her, truth is the same as falsehood and falsehood the same as truth. Often have I counselled a disciple to avoid women.

For months he left his father's second wife—the aunt who had reared him—at his door: she came each day, in rags, seeking a look or a kind word from him. It was only after years that he took the piety of women into consideration and agreed to the constitution of female communities.

The question was even asked whether women could reach Bodhi, and was the occasion of great debate between the Buddha and his disciples. After denying it the Master at last yielded to the insistence of his intimates, but he was not slow to repent it, for the nuns brought a disorder as much material as spiritual into their communities.

Hīnayāna and Mahāyāna agree in their expression of the disfavour in which women are held from the spiritual point of view. 'For this I have obtained a woman's body, because I have done wrong in a past life.'

A popular Tibetan text, translated by Bacot, is a good reflection of the Buddhist attitude of mind to woman. The context is a dialogue in which a monk explains to a girl why he keeps her out of his path:

> Women are the source of the three damnations.
> Traffic with women is the ruin of men.
> Women bring misfortune on men in this world and the next.
> There is no peace for a man who desires women.
> He who desires women must flee them. . . .
> Women are so clearly the source of all sin that Buddhas are not born of them. . . .
> The absolute and the relative, the void and mercy are realities that cannot be found together in women.
> This universe perishes because of their presence.

In the countries of the south woman still shows a meticulous discretion towards the monk. She should not touch the food when filling his alms-bowl, she should not tread on the rug or mat the monk is sitting on, she should never address him first, she should avoid uncovering herself before him, and she should sit in a posture that cannot awaken desire.

Communities of nuns eventually grew up in Annam, China, Cambodia, and Siam. The women have their skull and eyebrows shaved, dress in white or more rarely in yellow, and follow the monastic Rule. They administer themselves but are

e abbot of Lamaist monasteries is always a very learned man.
Doctor of Theology in the Buddhist University of Detsung. (Tibet.)

*Head and eyebrows shaved, the Buddhist nuns of Cambodia
weave their own robes and sashes.*

subject to moral supervision by the Abbot of a neighbouring masculine community.

The rule of celibacy has been respected for more than two thousand years. The monk must do nothing that might make him run the risk of losing his chastity: in principle he must not receive anything direct from a woman's hand; likewise if he goes on horseback, his mount must not be a mare. . . . Modern life has softened these ordinances a little, and today a monk may take his place in a vehicle or boat in which a woman is travelling: he will merely not speak to her, and turns his eyes away. Cambodian *bhikshus* hide their faces behind their fans in a woman's presence.

Yet celibacy is not followed by certain sects of Lamaist Buddhism, notably by the Sa-kya-pa (the 'Red' sect): far from being reprehensible, carnal intercourse is, as in certain sections of Hinduism, capable of leading to Enlightenment. The great reformer Tsong-Kha-pa was justly credited with re-establishing

With scrip in hand, the monk goes off to beg his sustenance,
his fan ready to hide the world from his eyes.

celibacy within the great Tibeto-Mongol sect of the Ge-luk-pa (known as the 'Yellow hats') which he founded.

In the *Prātimoksha*, the Buddha summed up the practical Rule in ten· prohibitions: the good Buddhist should abstain from stealing, killing, impure action, lying, drunkenness, eating after midday, interest in dancing, music or any entertainment, adorning himself with garlands and using scent, sleeping in high and broad beds, and accepting money.

Soon afterwards, two hundred and fifty prohibitions were added. Each month at the full and the new moon, the assembled *bhikshus* hear the Superior read the interminable list, and publicly confess their transgressions of them. Their repentance is marked by the lighting of little candles. It is noteworthy that blasphemy does not figure amongst the prohibitions, for there is no occasion to address oneself to any sacred dogma or personage.

The ordination of a *bhikshu* is a ceremony that starts with a triple entreaty by the neophyte's friends, not to give up the joys of life. After indicating refusal by his silence, the candidate undergoes questioning by a monk: 'Are you a woman? Are you impaired? Have you any debts? Have you a wife, or children? Do you believe in the transmigration of souls?' Then the hair of his head, eyebrows and body is shaven off, he is sprinkled with purifying water and his three garments and his personal objects are offered him on a tray. He accepts by touching them with a stick to show that he will no longer receive any object from hand to hand and that the offerings made him must henceforth be laid upon a table, on the ground or upon his fan. The ceremony concludes with a prayer that living and dead may benefit from the religious act of the new monk, who then pours a bowl of pure water on to the ground. His first act after this is to hear the 'Hundred and Eight evident Doors of the Law' which will be read to him by an Elder.

Apart from study and meditation, which are actually only practised by a small number, the principal occupations are represented by the common recitation of texts drawn from the scriptures, Sūtras and Śāstras, by the expounding of the Doctrine to the faithful on the eighth and fifteenth days of the waxing moon and by participation in religious festivals. These are very numerous, but the most important are the general Assemblies (*samgha-krama*), marking the boundary lines of consecrated lands, going into and coming out of retreat, and ordinations. Instructions laid down by the Superior are not to be discussed or interpreted. No vow of obedience has been taken, however, since the final aim remains the extinction of what we call our personality.

In general terms the monastery consists of some buildings, without any sort of sanctity, used as meeting-places and not thought to house a divinity. The monks hold their assemblies there, and come to hear the texts read. The faithful are admitted on set days to hear the Law preached and expounded. Neighbouring buildings house the library and serve for the reception of travellers.

Of course the *vihāras* have themselves undergone the external changes of Buddhism. What is inaccurately called the 'pagoda' has, in Siam, Cambodia, Laos, and even Ceylon instituted a

Between the services and the professional rounds,
the monks are allowed times of recreation when joy reigns unconstrained.

The monk must devote a part of his time
to meditation and the reading of the scriptures.
(Temple of Angkor, Cambodia.)

complicated architecture and a riot of frescoes, silver pavings, gold or jasper statues encrusted with precious gems. In Tibet, the harshness of the cold has made it necessary to build with thick walls, and the aspect of a monastery is that of a square fortress containing, as well as meeting-halls, libraries, and cells for meditation, all the subsidiary services necessary for self-supporting communities.

Except in the northern countries where the climate makes this sort of monastery life necessary, the monk is in the open air, only returning to the community's dwelling-places to sleep. During the monsoon rains he is at liberty to withdraw into joint convents (*vihāras*). Strictly speaking he should sleep sitting, with his back propped against a tree or the wall of his room, but this rule is not often observed. In any case he is recommended

101

not to shift his position unnecessarily. Once a month a night should be spent in a burial place to help him meditate on the vanity of human affairs.

Popular deviations have led the monk to join in secular life. He is present on the important occasions of life, he helps the dying to 'take the leap well', he tends the sick, for he has a smattering of medical knowledge. If called upon, as in Annam, Tibet, and Mongolia, he will read horoscopes and exorcise demons.

Buddhism cannot be summed up as simple communities following appreciably the same doctrine: it is a complete society in itself. Besides, contrary to what might be gathered from his teaching, the Buddha did not wish to found a contemplative Order. Energetic and militant like a true Kshatriya, he aimed at establishing a body always in action. Forbidding the idle life, he enjoined study, and preaching for one's neighbour's edification. Yet he did not wish to unite the communities under one control; rejecting the idea of appointing a successor, he exclaimed in entreaty to his favourite disciple:

> What, Ānanda! Does the Order of monks think that I shall not obtain absolute Nirvāna until I have left directions about this? I have taught the Dharma, Ānanda, without distinguishing between exoteric and esoteric; for where truths are concerned, Ānanda, the Finder of Truths does not keep his hand shut like the master who keeps back part of his knowledge. He does not think it is his part to be the head of the Order, or that the Order depends on him. Why, then, should I leave instructions?

He simply indicated that each monk had to be guided by the same preoccupations that had led him to inform the world of what he deemed it could understand. 'Accordingly, Māluñkyāputta, bear always in mind what it is that I have not elucidated, and what it is that I have elucidated.'

Following the Buddha's pattern of behaviour, the monk dispels his own ignorance and acquires compassion, without resentment against a Heaven from which he can expect no manifestation, succour or revelation, and without rebelling against the prison of rebirths; the adept has only to follow, and then teach, the plan of escape practised by the Sage. Finally, the solution that every monk must preach is that there exists only one remedy for the ills of life and death, and that is not to be reborn. 'Therefore, O Ānanda, you should continue on your way taking the Self as a lamp, the Self as a refuge and no other; taking the Dharma as a lamp, the Dharma as a refuge and no other.'

The existence of the Buddhist community, which has kept the original teaching intact, has thus preserved Buddhism. What brought about its social decline was the reawakening of Brahmanism, which made considerable borrowings from it, whilst echoing the popular taste for the marvellous; the return to the old fusion of the individual within the family, the caste, society; the acceptance by the monasteries of material gifts; and, lastly, a way of life and dress that exposed the monks, in times of invasion, to the savageries of war. It is conceivable that if coenobitism had not replaced the wandering life of the first enthusiasts Buddhism would not have been stamped out by the Mussulmans.

BUDDHISM IN INDIA

Neither the social strength which king Aśoka gave to Buddhism nor the councils could prevent dissension. Variations in the Doctrine, perhaps without affecting its ultimate basis, were codified. They certainly correspond to the differences in mentality and life of the southern and northern populations—whence the birth of the Hīnayāna and Mahāyāna schools.

In the damp, warm, debilitating climate of the lands of the south there is no room for dialectics or for the subtlety of controversies. Thus Ceylon, Burma and Cambodia will remain fairly faithful to the general principles set up in the fifth century B.C.

The Hīnayāna: The *Hina-yāna* (Little Vehicle) without doubt represents the highest expression of the original Buddhism and of a Triad whose terms are only meaningful when taken together:

1. the *Buddha*, Śākyamuni, historical personage, the primordial;
2. the *Dharma*, the Doctrine, the Word;
3. the *Saṃgha*, the Community, the creatures who follow the Law.

Whereas, as we shall see, the Mahāyāna moves amidst a pantheon, Hīnayāna does not believe in Bodhisattvas or in Buddhas, their existence not being proved.

As Conze has clearly shown, the line of demarcation is thus drawn, as in pure philosophy, between those (the Nominalists) for whom only the particular has real existence, and those who only consider the universal: the Hīnayānists only accepted a belief founded on a historical fact, whereas the Mahāyānists were content with the creatures of imagination without caring about possible incarnation in an historical personage.

Hīnayāna, therefore, accepted the evidence of pain and held that one could remedy it, although the process was difficult. Keeping to the pure primitive line of rejection of theological speculation, and refusing all esoteric interpretation, it clung less to the spirit than to the letter of the earliest writings. It made the abstraction of Nirvāṇa concrete as a paradise, and reserved a soul charged with karma to the individual. As for the Buddha, a miraculous power of being in all places at once was attributed to him. However, because of the easy living conditions that their climate offered southern Indians, the mystic's life that he had recommended was disregarded.

Hīnayāna developed above all in Ceylon: at Anurādhapura the ruins of one of the greatest Buddhist sanctuaries are still to be seen; at Kandy, where a tooth of Śākyamuni is revered, a university has been founded that has assembled an invaluable library.

Partisans of Hīnayāna and Mahāyāna have long continued in an opposition which had none of the Buddhist serenity: the former did not conceal the horror with which they regarded the introduction of Tantrism into the Doctrine; while those who stood by the Great Vehicle had the greatest scorn for the southern adepts, and used *hīna-yāna* as a term of abuse.

In Cambodia, Buddhism was divided into two sects: the MOHANIKAYS (Large Crowd, Skt. Mahā-nikāya) representing the old tradition brought from the south of India by the Kambojas, and the THOMAYUTS, who broke away from the former. This sect, also called 'Royal', claims a better understanding of the Texts and a stricter observance of the prescriptions.

The Mahayana: The name of *Mahā-yāna* (Great Vehicle) was assumed by the northern sect in contrast with the designation Little Vehicle.

The Mahāyāna preaches that man is not able to save himself from rebirths, during his sojourn on earth, by the Buddha's method alone. To be a Buddhist means to seek one's refuge in the Buddha, to turn one's soul towards some power capable of helping and saving; in other words, to appeal to divine mercy; and joined to this support, to make use of it so as to attain for oneself the wondrous state of the compassionate saviour. The final goal is entry into *Sukhāvatī*, the land of Bliss, where reigns the red 'Guardian of the West' AMITĀBHA.

These views had already been sketched out in the first two centuries after the Buddha's death, but they were rejected by the council of Pāṭaliputra in 245 B.C. Shortly before our era they regained strength in the India of the Ganges and expanded during the reign of Kanishka in the first century A.D. An enormous literature, in Sanskrit, was produced, less concerned with a reasoned approach than that of the Hīnayāna. Mention should be made of the *Lalita-Vistara*, a biography of Śākyamuni, the *Saddharma-puṇḍarika* or Lotus of the Good Law, and the monumental *Mahā-vastu* where the manner in which to realize the Bodhisattva ideal is set forth.

The Great Vehicle thus proves the work of commentators who, striving above all to bring out the spirit of the texts, claimed to be nearer to the Sage's real thoughts. It remained strictly monastic, of course, but slipped into speculation. This attitude was naturally bound to lead to such varied interpretations that the Doctrine suffered in the end not only proliferation but also important changes.

It was the Mahāyāna, with its blossoming from the second to the fifth centuries A.D., that encouraged the intrusion of Brahmanism; with Tantrism, the esoteric appeared. The great theorists—Nāgārjuna, Aśvaghosha, Āryadeva, Śāntideva—paved the way for a ŚAṄKARA, but it is debatable whether he adapted the Buddhist speculations of the first century A.D. to a new Brahmanism, or catalysed the invasion of Buddhism by metaphysics—condemned by the Buddha, as a newly established canon had just recalled.

Properly regarded, it is in the most ancient Vedic religion that Mahāyāna has its roots: it profited by this rich humus to invade Buddhism and give it a philosophical aspect.

The Mahāyāna, replacing the Brahmanic heavens by a Buddhist pantheon, deified popular creations, and so conferred on them a metaphysical character that went beyond mere fable. Hence the appearance of 'Buddhas of Meditation' (Dhyāni Buddhas)—in Sanskrit called the 'Victorious ones' (Jinas)—guardians of the five cardinal points, together with their spiritual reflections and earthly reflections.

Although distinct in names and provinces, the five Jinas—on the subject of which I shall have more to say when speaking of yogo-tantrism—are alike. They correspond to the Buddha in the supreme sense of the Absolute and at the same time they relate, through their attitudes (*āsanas*) and gestures (*mudrās*), to particular episodes of his enlightenment.

In their Transcendent 'Body' (Dharma-kāya), they have entered Nirvāṇa once for all, and no longer have any direct link with the world. This inaccessibility led to endowing them with two other forms: a Body of Bliss (*Saṃbhoga-kāya*), when as mediators for humanity (*bodhisattvas*) they can project a form to descend to earth, the Body of Emanation (*Nirmāṇa-kāya*).

Thus it is that the Dhyāni Buddha AMITĀBHA will have as his body of Bliss the Bodhisattva AVALOKITEŚVARA, who will despatch to earth his body of transformation SIDDHĀRTHA GAUTAMA, called

Mahāyāna Buddhism, which throve in the northern regions, is marked by the appearance, around the Buddha, of five 'Dhyānibuddhas', or buddhas of meditation. (China, T'ang period.)

ŚĀKYAMUNI. It is to be observed that the stem 'Īśvara' (Lord) is borrowed from Brahmanism, and corresponds to the human concept of an inconceivable Brahma.

Entering further into metaphysics, we find that the Dharma-kāya is the BODY OF THE LAW, impersonal and undifferentiated; it is not an ultimate aspect of reality but is beyond all manifestation. One can say of it that it 'simply is so, and no more' (*Bhūta-tathatā*). It might be likened to the flame of a fire that has gone out, which has not yet kindled another brand: it has entered a 'fire' Absolute which has never ceased to exist.

The Saṃbhogakāya, for its part, is the BODY OF BLISS, possessing name and form; personal and differentiated, it is a faultless body of manifestation. As for the Nirmāṇakāya, it is the BODY OF EMANATION or, if preferred, of incarnation. The union of the Transcendent Form with this body is no other than the Holy Spirit: it was in a human guise that the Buddha offered it to humanity.

Conditions of life being harder in the north and favouring seclusion and meditation, the Buddhist ideal showed greater scope. The individual, aided by the Buddha to whom he has entrusted himself, is no longer content with trying to be an arhat, a saint, but aims at nothing less than becoming a bodhisattva, and returning to earth to strive for human salvation and so attain buddhahood. The idea of making the greatest possible number of creatures benefit from a knowledge which will save them from the pain of endless transmigration follows that of the earliest Buddhism to the letter. 'When freed, free', taught the Sage. 'Having reached the other bank, help others to get there.'

The LOTUS OF THE GOOD LAW presents the world as a house on fire that the devotee wishes to flee by borrowing a vehicle. This means of salvation (*yāna*) is immense (*mahā*) and open to all. If the pure man who has grasped the four Truths is content with a goat-cart, he who wishes to penetrate causes and effects by himself will be drawn by a deer, whilst the adept desiring Nirvāṇa for all creatures will take his place in a carriage drawn by oxen: that man will show the same abnegation as the Master, who had

The bodhisattva Avalokiteśvara (with his multiple arms and heads, corresponding to different virtues and attributes) offers to the world the buddha Śākyamuni, his earthly incarnation. (Tibet.)

vowed not to enter the realm of Non-being before having enlightened the world.

There then developed the idea that man likewise could offer
the Perfect one and the bodhisattvas his devotion. The buddhas
prior to the birth of Siddhārtha were reckoned by the Hīnayānists at six: this number rose to twenty-four, and went on
increasing as the list was extended backwards, ending up with
a primal Buddha, Ādibuddha the Eternal.

Bhakti was broadened: the Dhyāni Buddha AKSHOBHYA (*The
Imperturbable*), who reigns in the east, long ranked higher than
AMITĀBHA (*infinite Light*) who rules the west. But the latter, with
his glorious counterpart AMITĀYUS (*infinite Life*), finally took first
place: in fact it was his spiritual son AVALOKITEŚVARA (*The Lord
who looks compassionately down*) and *his* earthly incarnation,
GAUTAMA ŚĀKYAMUNI, who undertook to save the world from
suffering.

One bodhisattva vies with Avalokiteśvara in popularity, viz.
MAÑJUŚRĪ, the personified deification of wisdom. A future
Buddha is foretold: MAITREYA, who will come down to earth to
finish the work of salvation in the period when man's span of
life has reached 80,coo years.

Setting out from the idea that, in the Mahāyāna Buddhism of
faith, if all have a right to salvation, all must have the same
access to it, the literature concerned itself with establishing
formulae to approach the deities. Prayers were devised, painted
or sculptured representations were objects of adoration, and a
ceremonial of worship was established.

It is undeniable that these material practices have nothing in
common with the Bhagavat's revelation. Similarly, the implacable book-keeping of karma is qualified by the possibility
of intercession. But all the same it is admissible to assume the
truth of the Buddha's saying, 'The actions of saints can inspire
the crowd.' The widening of the bhaktic trend allows the cor-
rection of such egoism as might arise from exaggerated concentration on the pursuit of one's own salvation.

To give oneself up to Faith rather than seeking Deliverance

for one's self, on the other hand, involved the recognition of the futility and vanity of personal power. Perfection and salvation do not depend on one's unaided efforts but rather on the gifts of someone else: a great lesson in modesty, sincerity, and purity that shows perfection is only encountered at the very moment when its image is quenched, when there is no more consciousness of merit or feeling of emptiness.

Under these conditions the Buddhist renounces. commitment and a desire for Non-existence. He contents himself with patiently pursuing the obliteration of the ego and the craving to live. Detached from everything and from himself, he diffuses his existence before thinking of Nirvāṇa. His ideal is to be a bodhisattva, a saviour through 'pure love of living beings'.

From the fifth to the eighth century A.D., the Mahāyāna spread towards Nepal, Tibet, China, and then Japan. In the last two countries, it only impregnated the masses without claiming to form the basis of a national cult. On the other hand, in cold countries such as Tibet and Mongolia it sank deep, for meditation, ill-suited to the open air, requires hermitages; the importance of the ascetic life is shown in the number of monasteries and this serves as an influential example. A dichotomy was effected, however, between the people and a fraternity in which it took nothing like the part it did in the southern regions. If there was any participation, it was directed and controlled by the great monasteries.

The influence of these organizations was reinforced by the fact that the monks passed beyond spiritual power, the superiors or abbots being incarnations of bodhisattvas. It is only thanks to this sanctity that the Doctrine could be grafted on to the primitive cults without damage. It is seen, then, coming to terms with animism, with demonology and deep-rooted social tenets.

Whilst Hīnayāna and Mahāyāna were in agreement over the Third Truth—the suppression of desire and ignorance in order to obtain Nirvāṇa—the Little Vehicle, falling short of Buddhism, denied universal salvation; whereas the Great Vehicle conceived a speculative metaphysics of Abhidharma and believed in an apostolic proselytism. Ending by adoring what the Buddha had done away with—God, the soul, rites and liturgy—it finished up as deity worship.

Buddhism was thus to lose by degrees what distinguished it from Brahmanism. By introducing the metaphysical with its popular appeal, it made way for nascent Vishṇuism and Śivaism: Brahman, the One and the Absolute of the traditional mysticisms alone remained absent from what was henceforth to be named 'The Religion' (Dharma). A sect among sects, it yet survived by the considerable force of its negations, and even succeeded in persisting for a long time in a society subject to the Brahmins.

Salvation: Mahāyāna took final shape in the second century A.D. and reached its culmination under the impetus of Nāgarjuna, the thirteenth patriarch. This master, probably the most eminent after the Sage himself, claimed to have found in a cave the authentic writings entrusted to the care of the Nāgas by the Buddha.

A NEW SCHOOL OF WISDOM arose, which can be summed up in three negations:

Non-attainment or Self-extinction

Non-assertion

Non-relying, to avoid the extreme anxiety of adherence; and one affirmation:

to become *omniscient*.

It is impossible to gain Nirvāṇa so long as one makes a distinction between it and oneself, between the object to be gained and a former state one remembers. Still to be conscious of even the highest virtue immediately debases it: to know that one has reached the acme of humility engenders pride which automatically refutes it.

It is impossible to gain Nirvāṇa while uttering a question or assertion; the man who has realized Emptiness can no longer have any positive or negative attitude about what it is. 'For' or 'against' are terms unknown to the Sage.

It is impossible to attain Nirvāṇa without having got rid of the anxiety which forces us to hold on to something different from ourselves. So long as one support remains, the whole task has yet to be accomplished.

What the Mahāyānist hopes for from the greater of the Vehicles is the omniscience of the buddhas, who know every aspect of the world in the least detail. Could not the Sage state the number of all the insects alive at any given instant? Not the earthly Buddha, of course, nor even his 'glorious form', but his spiritual principle, his 'Dharma Body'. This dialectic makes it clear that Nāgārjuna sought not to come to any definite conclusion but rather to reduce all positive beliefs to absurdity. There is no need to point out that his teaching was only intended for trained Buddhists.

Mysticism: The Buddha did not seek to bring about an improvement in the state of mankind. Nor did he go into practical details of the experience he had successfully undergone, or reveal what his Enlightenment had brought him. He merely taught that Wisdom can free, a wisdom within reach of anyone who wishes to acquire it.

But wisdom is not merely good conduct according to a rule; it does not consist of the making of reflections and conclusions drawn by the intellect from the experience of life. It can only be gained at the end of a long and laborious detachment, in all-but-complete forgetfulness of the world: matter, sensation, and feeling. The sole way of salvation is asceticism, a door opened on mysticism which allows contact with the intangible.

It is obvious that the Doctrine here loses the strict idea of a Karma depending on one's acts. When we read in the Bhagavad-Gītā 'To believe that I am the agent or that so-and-so is the agent, that I or so-and-so shall reap what we have sown, is to pass by the truth,' we must understand a certain determinism as the cause of our actions.

Asceticism allows one to grasp that there exists only one reality, that of the immutable and eternal. Anything that depends on a cause is only real by virtue of connections with things or beings different from itself. This distinction is indispensable if we are to understand what has been termed subject and object, and not let illusion confuse them.

Thus the image of ourself that we see in a mirror is a projection of our person, devoid of independent existence. It is empty of all substance and without any absolute reality. Further, the examination of what the mirror reflects, apart from ourself, shows us only one aspect of the world, just what the reflecting surface happens to catch. Shift this, and one becomes aware of other aspects. One cannot then discover all at once the totality of the world's aspect by examining a mirror. But what is our eye, if not a mirror? A mirror, moreover, that is incapable of self-experience? Who has heard of an eye capable of looking at itself? That is not what it perceives in the glass.

Prajñā: Consequently, our consciousness, being a phenomenon, will itself be an obstacle to any Enlightenment. By contrast, a temporarily unconscious subject, *Prajñā*, represents the faculty, which we possess and can develop, of receiving Enlightenment. For all its resemblance to that Ātman which the Buddha had denied as identifying itself with Brahman, it is *not* immediate Knowledge, without subject-object duality. It is 'Pre-Wisdom'. It is best understood by a comparison with the geotaxis and phototaxis of a seed, which, when it germinates, orients its radicle towards the earth and its stem towards the light.

Mahāyāna is thus seen to have made concrete a mysticism without divine intervention. If an actual, permanent element 'really' exists in us, it can only be revealed to us by the progressive abolition of what is alien to it, i.e. of that which we regard as our individuality. We have no consciousness of it and will only know it at the moment when our consciousness is wholly abolished. There is, it is plain, a great difference from the search for a relationship with the divine as the yogins understood it: purification, rites, rejection of all that masks Divinity, endeavour to penetrate to it by breaking down all the barriers behind which it waits and hopes to be discovered.

The Element of Consciousness: The Buddha taught us that besides earth, water, air, fire, and space there exists a sixth element, the ELEMENT OF CONSCIOUSNESS (the *Vijñānadhātu*), which establishes the relationship between two successive existences. It has been likened to a flame which, dying, lights another: 'like the transmission of learning from teacher to disciple, like the lighting of a lamp from another lamp or like the impress of a stamp on wax' (Dasgupta). The effect becomes a cause in its turn.

The Mahāyāna replaced this element by that of UNIVERSAL CONSCIOUSNESS (Ālaya-vijñāna) without modifying the idea of an unconscious continuity. All Vijñāna disappears before Knowledge through Illumination, but not beyond death. At least, the Buddha said nothing about it. But, in the QUESTIONS OF MILINDA the sage Nāgasena declares: 'When the light has gone out after the scribe has written a letter, the letter still exists. Likewise, when Wisdom has disappeared, the knowledge it has aroused persists.'

The present-day Buddhist commentator Ananda Coomaraswamy shows with masterly clarity that in the doctrine of causality, as in that of the causal effect of actions (karma), there is nothing that necessarily entails a 'reincarnation' of souls. The doctrine of causality is common to Buddhism and Christianity; each religion explicitly proclaims its belief in an ordered sequence of events. This 'reincarnation' of which the Buddhist would like to be rid is not the accident of a particular death nor of a particular rebirth hoped for in the future: it is the whole dizzy process of dying and being reborn many times, which characterizes, equally, existence here in the human condition and existence on high, lasting eternities, in the divine.

Time involves movement, and movement change of place; in other words, duration brings mutation, and 'becoming'. That is why the immortality envisaged by the Buddhist is not spatial or temporal but independent of time and space.

So it is confirmed that Nirvāṇa is not Nothingness. Nevertheless it reveals itself as non-personal: the desire of a conscious after-life would be a bond with existence that would prevent any deliverance. This estimate tallies well with the words of the Gospel: 'For whosoever will save his life shall lose it.'

None of these conceptions affords any foothold for the intellect, and it is understandable that the Blessed one avoided all precise statement. Intuition alone allows one to appreciate the depth of the reply made by Śāriputra to those who questioned him on what had become of the Buddha after his entry into Nirvāṇa: 'There is, monks, an unborn, not become, not made, uncompounded. Were it not for that, there would be no escape for the born, the become and the compounded.'

The Prajñāpāramitā: This term (Prajñā-pāram-i-tā) which means literally the *Beyond-gone-ness of Wisdom* (Prajñā), in other words its complete attainment, synthesizes the whole work of Nāgārjuna.

A latent veiled wisdom lies dormant within us in unconsciousness and ignorance. Disperse this ignorance and we are in a state to receive that light, just as after a long sleep peopled with dreams the individual returns to 'real' life. Consequently the Buddhist must above all discard and suppress whatever hides the truth from him.

Prajñā is recognized as soon as the world of phenomena is left, when there is no longer any duality between subject and object. Enlightenment thus presents a positive, metaphysical character, whereas Nirvāṇa, by the suppression of suffering and affliction, could be defined as negative and affective.

Emptiness: The name of Prajñā-pāramitā was given to a part of the hundred or so volumes that make up the canonical works of the Great Vehicle. It deals particularly with Emptiness, and to render this notion more approachable it was summed up in a catechism where the bodhisattva Avalokiteśvara (the Mediator) and Śāriputra (Wisdom) established the theory of universal emptiness, which Foucher very rightly calls the 'Fifth Truth'.

When one reaches the idea of the Void, one is obliged to revise the first assessment one may have made of Mahāyāna: far from being a 'Middle Way' and moderate, the Great Vehicle is extreme in its nihilism; in fact it denies the personality and the elements composing it, as well as phenomena and causality. In the end it made a religion of what the Buddha had evaded, the Void. Its commentators, for that matter, called themselves *Śūnyavādins*—nihilists or deniers.

> The Buddha hath the causes told
> Of all things springing from a cause;
> And also how things cease to be—
> 'Tis this the Mighty Monk proclaims.

The Void (*śūnya*) is not nothingness, and Emptiness (*śūnyatā*) can be thought of as non-substance, non-existence, relative reality. The arhat does not say 'I am not' but 'I am nothing.'

What may be understood by the Void is shown in the reply made by the Buddha to Śāriputra:

Where there is form (*rūpa*) there is the void, and where the void is, there is form. Void and form are therefore not distinct.

The five elements (*skandha*) have the character of the void. They are not born, nor do they come to an end, they neither increase nor diminish, they are neither pure nor impure.

In the void, O Śāriputra, there is neither form, sensation, idea, volition nor consciousness. In the void, there are neither eyes, nor ears, nor nose, nor tongue, nor body, nor mind. In the void there is neither colour, nor sound, nor smell, nor taste, nor touch, nor elements. In the void there is neither ignorance nor knowledge nor even cessation of ignorance. In the void are neither pain, nor grief, nor obstacles, nor road; neither old age nor death. In the void is no Knowledge or obtaining of Knowledge.

Achievement of Prajñāpāramitā: The practices aim at the acquisition of more or less direct intuitive cognition, without the least pressure from a mind concentrating on a desired achievement: no effort can succeed if it acts upon anything but the removal of obstacles. Transcendental meditation is not an intellectual game of setting out to explore: it carries men away.

To understand the weakness of our mental apparatus better,

we have only to gauge our difficulties in approaching measures which are not on our scale. What in fact do the micron and the light-year represent, if not that a molecule is infinitely small, or a star infinitely distant? In mathematics we deal with differential calculus, imaginary number, the quantum or curved space, although the intellect can only conceive of them in abstractions.

Only the knowledge of what can be and is realized, is valid. To 'realize' the Void, then, is to separate phenomena into their constituent elements, which will then cease to be, for want of a unifying factor.

It follows that one can become buddha during one's lifetime if one disperses the opposing forces. To analyse phenomena into their constituent elements is to take action against these forces. All the possibilities of illusion will be exhausted by piercing at one stroke to the centre of the Void and not by discovering them one by one: exactly as a mirage is dispersed when one dives straight into the vision in an aeroplane.

Sainthood is only a stage. The arhat subjugates his sensations, does away with his feelings of joy, sorrow, sympathy and antipathy, attractions and repulsions. The individual is now only considered as he is, cut off from all subjectivity. Analysis yields only memories, images—in a word, forces. By their persistence and ever possible return, they render the state of sainthood precarious and vulnerable, if there is lack of courage, or Grace is wanting.

It is no use the adept's renouncing whatever reassurance there may be in personal and conscious efforts; in vain he rids himself of pride, of intellect and heart; he may even have acknowledged that no merit and no wisdom can grant privileges, and given himself up to the stream of salvation; yet all this is of no avail if at the last moment the grace of the Absolute does not come to extinguish the image of perfection at the very instant it is reached: buddhahood only manifests itself when it is no longer discernible.

The mystical texts of Mahāyāna are only a form of mnemonic: their sense is infinitely more complex than the simple written

Prajñāpāramitā sunk in inner contemplation of Wisdom.
(Javanese work, bronze.)

words. The Buddhist who devotes himself to asceticism can only succeed in penetrating his 'real' inner universe and eliminating Self after an initiation at the hands of a master 'skilful at pointing out errors'. The disciple's experience is ordered, directed and controlled by the guide. As the Water Śāstra teaches: 'If one watered the hundred leaves of a withered tree a hundred times they would never again turn green.'

THE EVOLUTION OF THE LAW

When the Buddha entered Nirvāṇa, his Doctrine had only influenced an *élite*: and even among them, only a meagre proportion of the Brahmins and Kshatriyas living in Magadha and the principalities in its immediate vicinity. As for the people, only those Vaiśyas and Śūdras who had been directly moved at first hand by a sermon of the Blessed one had been converted. So, in spite of the Master's forty years' wanderings, the number of supporters at his death can scarcely be reckoned at more than a few tens of thousands.

Certainly the influence of King Aśoka was considerable, and one can say that under his rule and that

of his immediate successors the peninsula had been won over to Buddhist gentleness and spirituality. But even more than the efforts of a great monarch making use of his power to elevate his people, it was legend that spread Buddhism throughout India. Around the accounts of miracles places of pilgrimage were organized, and, in their turn, the monasteries that were built there shaped the legends. There are two great centres around which such accounts gravitate: Bodh-gayā, where the Enlightenment took place under the fig-tree, and Benares, which had admittedly been a sacred city where a hundred sects jostled each other long before the Sage preached.

The Buddha corresponds to the archetype of the magical hero, and the inexhaustible thirst for the miraculous attributed to him divine and supernatural qualities. He had struggled, and so well had he triumphed, it seems, that the Brahmins themselves had turned from their gods to come and pay him homage. It is easy to imagine that within a century the belief spread through the entire peninsula that a deity had made himself man to come and teach men the way to happiness in this life. And to prove that he came straight down from heaven, this Saviour had performed miracles, which, by oral tradition, multiplied and became more and more astonishing.

Aśoka at one and the same time checked the development of extravagant myths and made it possible for Buddhism to penetrate the masses. What had until then been only a distant speculation of elect disciples—and of disciples of these disciples—became accessible to the people. Largely thanks to the monks of the Mahāsamghika sect, the teaching became more concrete, and insisted more upon the doctrine of Karma and rebirth: the Dharma, Self-extinction, and Nirvāṇa yielded to very rationalist conceptions—which by no means betrayed the words of the Blessed one: 'To accept nothing that was not verified or proved.'

This popularization met with success only at the price of counter-concessions in paradoxical contradiction with such subjection to scrutiny. Only the appearance of a new, more powerful god could reconcile the people to the dethronement of their ancient deities. A century after Aśoka, the Buddha was adored under his humanized form, and a popular literature was created, in which nothing precise about the Community of monks is found, but which contains an exaltation of moral virtues desirable as regards Karma, and backed up by miraculous stories. The layman's imagination was appealed to in order to strengthen his devotion.

According to the angle from which it is examined, Buddhism can consequently be regarded under two aspects:

(1) The Buddhism taught by the Buddha: distorted as it may have been already in the earliest scriptures, it presents features whose authenticity is beyond dispute. It appears to us as negative, *a*-religious and *a*-theistic (this *a*- privative must not be confused with 'anti-', for the Buddha's silences cannot be taken for denials). We have already seen that the Hīnayāna sect allows us to picture its primitive form.

(2) A Buddhism in evolution, speculative, to be invaded by resurgent Brahminism. From the outset the theorists stated what the Buddha had deliberately refused to impart, or had only offered poetically in a blurred form; or finally had really been unable to teach for want of the possibility of sufficiently precise verbal expression, of spiritual maturity amongst his disciples, and perhaps too of the necessary time. It may even be supposed that the Sage deemed no approach to Enlightenment possible on ground that had been too well cleared. If we rid it of its proliferous mythology, Mahāyāna demonstrates in its enormous literature the considerable effort undertaken to interpret what the Buddha meant to say and what he was silent about. All one is sure of concerning his teaching is that, like the plant which seeks to dispel the darkness in order to gain the light, it was undoubtedly clearer on what must be shunned than on what must be sought.

The Yogācārins: Whilst the OLD SCHOOL OF WISDOM had regarded Nirvāṇa as absolutely opposed to the world, whilst the OLD MAHĀYĀNA in Prajñāpāramitā identified Nirvāṇa and this world in one absolute reality, emptiness, and whilst the NEW

SCHOOL OF WISDOM saw emptiness as the only valid reality, the adherents of the YOGĀCĀRA identified this emptiness with thought: besides thought, nothing exists in the outside world.

Up to the end of the second century B.C. the monks cared little what the universe was. Reality was only a succession of events (*Abhidharma*), and all that counted for self-knowledge were the mental states and the psychological methods.

Around the year A.D. 180 there arose a sect, whose text was the ABHISAMAYĀLAMKĀRA, which applied itself to an explanation of the Prajñāpāramitā. Its adepts were the true precursors of the Yogācāra, which was founded in opposition to the Abhidharma by Asaṅga and Vasubandhu, two brothers of north-west Indian origin.

To understand the very complex thesis of this school it is necessary to refer to the *Bhagavad-Gītā*, that magnificent poem of the Lion of the Mahā-Bhārata. We find there—with the means for refuting them—the exposition of the philosophical methods and systems then current: Vedānta, Sāṃkhya, Yoga. In particular, it regards these last two as practically the contrary of the original Buddhist doctrine.

Whereas the 'Men of Wisdom', intellectuals devoted to the Dharma (*Mādhyamikas* and *Sarvāstivādins*) are led by way of *insight* to Enlightenment, the 'Men of Trance', chiefly ascetics and contemplatives, can equally reach this Enlightenment—but by mental concentration alone. There is nothing exclusive about this: wisdom suits some better, and trance others, according to temperament.

Asaṅga and Vasubandhu represented a reaction against the over-emphasis of a thought-process, with its consequent neglect of trance practices.

For the Yogācārins there is only thought, this thought being in actual fact defined as a state of 'transparent' luminosity: the Absolute is thus Thought, and it must not be sought in any object but in the pure subject, freed of all objects. We here meet again the fundamental opposition and the incompatibility between object and subject that we have already mentioned. Directly one turns towards the subject it becomes an object and loses its character of observer. No introspection therefore allows contact with a subject which thus modifies itself at once.

The Yogācārins set out to prove the error of regarding any thing as separated from the Self (or opposed to the Self) and presented to our examination in the rôle of an object.

All things and all thoughts can be expressed by 'Mind only'. There exists in the world a point of consciousness, a certain infinitely small dimension of *self-awareness* which the yogin can reach at the very moment when, in the course of trance, he comes to understand that these visions are no more hallucinatory than what he called realities in his waking state. 'Just as one perceives the lack of objectivity in the dream pictures after one has woken up, so the lack of objectivity in the perceptions of waking life is perceived by those who have been awakened by the knowledge of true reality.' (Asaṅga, quoted by Conze.)

Nirvāṇa may thus be described as *Mind-Only*, *Thought-Only*, or *Consciousness-Only*. Here we see stated the deviation from the original Buddhism which defined Nirvāṇa as 'a blowing out'.

Although dedicated to Vishṇu, the Bhagavad-Gītā cannot be disowned by any Yogācārin.

You bear in yourself a sublime friend whom you do not know. This God abides within every man, but few know how to find him. The man who sacrifices his desires and his works to the Being from whom the principles of all things proceed and by whom the universe' was shaped obtains perfection by this sacrifice. For he who finds in himself his gladness, his joy, and in himself also his light, is one with God. Now know that the soul which has found God is delivered from rebirth and from death, from old age and from pain, and drinks the water of immortality.

Henceforth, with this Yogācāra, which is echoed in the Tantric Buddhism of Tibet, it is universal salvation that is sought. Mental states are now only envisaged as bound up with the Cosmos.

The decline of Buddhism in India: After undergoing great development around the fifth century A.D., Yogācāra disappeared from India about 1100. It emigrated to Tibet and to China where some scattered elements of it are still found today, though without the survival of the transcendent logic with which DIÑ-NĀGA had marked the apogee of the sect.

Buddhism has a double aspect at this period: a development of sainthood and an increasing orientation towards intellectualism. Some centuries after the Buddha's death the saints are reckoned in thousands. Every monk, if he has the courage to detach himself from the world, may hope to become an arhat. Even the humble believers are capable of union with the Dharma through trance. There was a comparable development in erudition, until it took the place of the supreme attainment: it was the age of Doctors of the Law. Soon the meticulous work of exegesis would obscure the great primal rules of Buddhism preached by the Sage.

The Doctrine could not in fact escape the law of impermanence. In India it was steadily submerged by a Brahmanism which Buddhism had slightly altered. Moreover, the points in common which favoured the resurgence of the old religions were numerous: the illusion of individuality, the contingent nature of right and wrong, the possibility of being delivered from rebirths during an earthly life; Knowledge also, as the supreme end of all evolution, and even the conception of a Nirvāṇa—this becoming more definite than at the start. Brahmanists and Mahāyānists believed in saviours, freed human beings who returned to earth out of compassion for others. Northern Buddhism for its part inclined towards the acceptance of a heaven peopled with metaphysical beings, the Jinas, and even kept the name of Brahmā—applying it to a divine being though without granting him the power to break the cycle of rebirths.

It was not all a matter of reconciliation, however. Brahmanist thought, so well expressed in the Bhagavad-Gītā, exalted action and considered it efficacious if it was disinterested. The denial of the existence of the soul, so long a corner-stone of Buddhism, was in the end dialectically revised.

It may indeed be thought strange that, after the first burst of novelty, Brahminical India did not immediately begin to get the better of Buddhism. Gaining considerable ground thanks to

Aśoka, the Law set going a fundamental overthrow of social architecture. Even more than Brahmanism, Buddhism was a means of uniting a fragmented civilization always seething with rivalries. It was supported by the petty princes, who at first saw in it only a way of weakening the Brahmin caste, and later the resolution of some governmental difficulties. The exercise of kingship was no longer in danger of criticism from the masses who, persuaded that this world had absolutely no importance, were ready to accept all oppressions. Even if the 'Buddhistic' peoples had not already come to regard all evil as unavoidable, even necessary, the non-violence preached by the Buddha would alone have sufficed to prevent any revolt.

All India ought therefore to have been won over to Buddhism, for it was not 'against' the ancient cults. Yet it declined when, as a result of wars, its royal adherents lost their territories to Brahmanist sovereigns. Its universal nature gradually appeared to the Indians as a menace towards a kind of diffuse nationalism which had always united the various peoples of the peninsula. As Brahmanism had spontaneously or out of policy relaxed the strictness of certain of its principles, and Buddhism had on its side accepted out of tolerance the continued existence of the ancient predilections of the masses, the general adoption of the Doctrine could only peter out in India. What the Buddha's message to humanity actually represented was to be increasingly worn away through contact with the more ancient attachments of the people. About the year A.D. 400, Vasubandhu concluded his TREASURE OF ABHIDHARMA with a cry of alarm: 'The religion of the Sage is at its last breath; this is an age in which vice is powerful; those who want to be delivered must be diligent.'

Whilst the southern populations remained Buddhist in little more than name and left the practice of the Law to the bhikshus, the missionary zeal of the preachers and the part played in commercial relations by the Buddhists, who unlike the Brahmins were not hindered by rules of caste and were able to travel freely and spread the Doctrine, gave the spiritual lead to foreign populations.

The fundamental tolerance of Buddhism did not give it the air of a rival religion. Not only did it allow all cults but it could even come to terms with them. As it adapted itself to local ways and helped in the unification of heterogeneous peoples, foreign kings so favoured it that many of their number were regarded as bodhisattvas. Does not a fourteenth-century Uighur inscription refer to Genghis Khan, of all people, as the incarnation of such a bodhisattva? Did not Mongka, the third great Mongol Khan, compare Buddhism to the palm of the hand of which other cults—Nestorian, Islamic, or Taoist— were the fingers?

126

Outside India, therefore, we shall meet forms of Buddhism
extremely characteristic of the countries where it was adopted:
its universality, its indifference to the world and its realism
allowed it to be taken over without ceasing to be attached to the
Four Great Truths—thanks to apparent capitulations or at least
appreciable divergences from those sermons which, in the fifth
century B.C., brought men the opportunity of escaping from
their painful prison of repeated existences.

According to the Elders, however, all was not yet over. Certain sages, around 200 B.C., had foreseen the decline of the Law
in the centuries that were to come. But time itself is only a
fiction; the over-riding principle is ceaseless change, and in the
evolutionary course of the universe the farthest swings of the
pendulum only appear as infinitesimal waverings. After night
comes day; the shadow that has spread disappears before the
returning light.

And so there are formal prophecies which, from the reign of
Aśoka, equate the vitality of the Buddhist Doctrine with the
average span of human life. They anticipate that this will
steadily decrease to ten years—corresponding to a total forget-
ting of the Law—and then rise again to eighty thousand. At
this period the earth will be covered with a golden sand, so fertile that it will yield seven harvests a year; humanity, now
naturally increased in number, will be moral and virtuous. Then
the Buddha Maitreya will descend from the Tushita Heaven
to preach, and those who hear him will obtain Nirvāṇa merely
by doing so.

Without waiting for this proof of the ultimate glorification of
Buddhism, we can still see that the Buddha was justified in the
reliance he placed on man's keeping well away from extremes:
whatever the sect concerned, Hīnayāna, Mahāyāna, Tantric
Buddhism, Chinese Ch'an, and Japanese Zen, we find that the
Buddhists have never in actual fact departed from the proper
mean. As Coomaraswamy pertinently recalls, 'The true walk
with God is a middle way.' The Sage's earthly life was an
example: brought up in pleasure, luxury and unconcern and

127

then almost dying from the mortifications he inflicted on his body, 'the Master understood that neither the one nor the other of these extremes would lead him to the Knowledge he was seeking and which he obtained by following the middle Way.'

Purity is not obtained through virtue, any more than without it.

NON-INDIAN BUDDHISM

THE TIBETO-MONGOL BUDDHIST PANTHEON

Tantric Buddhism: Giving way before the ashen trident with which the devotees of Vishṇu mark their foreheads, and the red spot drawn between the eyebrows of the Śivaites, Buddhism, still animated by a universalism which had something to offer all men whatever their race or creed, slipped by degrees out of India. But although it was fading out in the peninsula, the speculative and theistic deviation of the Mahāyāna would take firm root abroad. It offered the masses the chance of jumping aboard some great vehicle which would carry them towards a luminous Non-being. Without becoming the more the leaders of men, the monks made themselves the representatives of a propitiatory priesthood introduced between man and the Cosmos. In Tibet, Mongolia, and China rituals were established, strict knowledge of which was reserved to specialists in performance and formulae. These men recognized the utility of recitations, asceticism, and even of magic. From what had been a morality, a social and internal way of behaviour, a will to do good in order not to weigh down one's karma, from all that represented the effort to break the chain of rebirths, were born a Buddhist religion, cults and schisms.

Without denying the impermanence of the soul, a kind of compromise was accepted: it is thus that the Tibetans look upon a succession of lives as the separate flowers of a garland hung on a single thread: this is the *ekotibhava* ('The Being threaded together').

Yet, in this expansion, Buddhism kept the indeterminacy of Nirvāṇa intact. The doctors had not been able to agree on a definition of this mystical state wherein all phenomenal consciousness on the human scale ceases: this very imprecision was to allow the Doctrine to adapt itself to its new adoptive countries.

Buddhism entered them laden with contributions from Indian

Buddhist festivities in a Tibetan monastery.

thought: those that had constituted the ancient stock upon which it had been grafted, and those that entered it after some modification. The monk Asanga had introduced the practice of yoga into the Law, referring to the mental concentration and control of the body that had allowed the Buddha to enter into ecstatic union with a universe which abruptly disclosed itself in a dazzling revelation. The *Tantras* (manuals) dedicated to Śiva brought forward the notion of a primordial Eternal Being.

Tantrism represents rather a doctrinal mode than an independent doctrine. As it establishes connections and analogies between man and the universe, between microcosm and macrocosm, the intuitive faculties on which it is based have conferred on it an essentially empirical character. It may be suggested that it enters the domain of magic, but if so, it is the highest magic.

After Nāgārjuna's time, the Buddhist monks of India were not content to practise and preach the teaching of an Enlightened one who had earned release from being reborn; they allowed the masses to worship the Sage as a deity who had existed for all time, member of an immense cosmic family that devolved entirely on him; without realizing it, the people rediscovered in him the Persian solar myths, more appealing in the state of an eternally living deity than a saviour dead for ever.

Finally, about the sixth century A.D., the mysticism of the Sivaite cult was definitely grafted upon Buddhism. The Brahmanist gods who had resumed their place and the bodhisattvas themselves were provided with consorts and wives: their active energy being materialized under a feminine form, the *śakti*. Perfect knowledge and the Absolute, the compassionate desire to save and intuitive wisdom, are powerless one without the other—exactly as man and woman can only create in the union of their substance.

'Good words' were to replace 'good actions'. The repetition countless times of OM MAṆI-PADME HŪM! (Jewel-in-the-Lotus) would be enough to lay one's heart at the feet of the Buddha. The name Mahāyāna made way for that of MANTRA-YĀNA (way of Invocations) or VAJRA-YĀNA (way of the Thunderbolt or the

Diamond). Deities and bodhisattvas, incomplete fragments of the universal soul (VAJRA-SATTVA), were endowed with various attributes—hence with varied dispositions. They were conceived as sometimes tranquil and welcoming, sometimes fierce and hostile. Since the malevolent aspect was by definition less favourable to mankind than the mild, it was accordingly held in especial veneration. From the benevolent as well as from the terrible, miracles and boons were expected. Perhaps it was this paradoxical combination of a spiritual assertion with a magical submission to the worshipper's own interests that allowed, from the second century B.C., the conversion of so many diverse peoples to Buddhism.

Buddhism in Tibet: It was in this form, then, that there penetrated to Tibet in the seventh century A.D. the Yogo-Tantric Buddhism that we wrongly name *Lamaism*, whereas the Tibeto-Mongols only know their belief under the designation, pure and simple, of 'THE RELIGION'. It was introduced by the two wives of the Tibetan king Song-tsen Gam-po, one Nepalese and the other Chinese, who vied with one another to propagate the Buddhist faith in which they had been brought up in their respective countries. When they died, a tear fell upon them from the middle eye of the eleventh head of the bodhisattva Avalokiteśvara, and testified that they were no other than the archangel's incarnations. Subsequently they were to be honoured under the name of the WHITE TĀRĀ and the GREEN TĀRĀ, protectresses of Tibet.

Illiterate, polyandrous and savage, sometimes cannibals, the Tibetans had from time immemorial built up a firm belief in spirits—in evil spirits, of course, corresponding to the frightful climate, a geography of unequalled harshness, and a mentality essentially primitive and particularly subject to the unconscious. The young Doctrine—though it was nearly twelve hundred years old already—had to ally itself with necromancy. The renunciation of all passion, and the Noble Eightfold Path leading to the abolition of pain, were found side by side with the most gruesome images of death and of the terrors of the beyond. Enriched with all the archetypes that humanity forged in its infancy and preserves buried under the surface, the cult of a wise, realistic Buddha enlightened with Knowledge flourished among demons and furious goddesses; he became the Supreme master of all the gods. Buddhism, conquered as much as conquering, accepted the raising up of deities belonging to a more and more complicated pantheon, admitted the identification of the adept with the god prayed to, and attempted to dominate the forces of nature. Sometimes it became bloodthirsty and obscene. It did not reject the salvation of woman through sexual union with a saint—always provided that he took no pleasure in it.

The pioneers: Buddhism was introduced into Tibet by some monks brought back by an emissary that the king's Nepalese wife had sent to India. A struggle began. Apart from the violent reaction of the sorcerers of the demonolatrous P'ön-po (*Bon-po*) religion, the Tibetans remained distrustful and only accepted a Doctrine blended with reprehensible beliefs.

In the year 747 a red-hatted yogin arrived from Kashmir, land of renowned magicians. His name was PADMA-SAMBHAVA, the 'Lotus-born'. Armed only with his ardour, the Vajra (Tib. Dorje) or thunderbolt, Indra's elephant-goad and the eight magical powers (the eight *siddhis*), he summoned all the Invisible beings hostile to the Law. He influenced the soul of some, smashed the power of others by means of the dorje and terrified the remainder. Enrolling the heavenly host and the legions of hell as Defenders of The Religion, the 'Very Precious Master' (*guru rin-po-che*) founded an order and built the first Tibetan monastery on the banks of the Brahmaputra. When, fifty years later, he returned to his own land, he left a solid nucleus of disciples to whom he had taught the Doctrine as well as the magic to defend it with.

There were apostasies, and persecutions. But Buddhism reflowered in 1031 with the arrival of the Bengali monk ATISA, who reformed errors by subjecting the teachings to the meticulous scholasticism of the Mahāyāna. From the order he founded, numerous sub-sects afterwards arose and codified extravagant notions in a spirit of quarrelsome rivalry. The Religion had regained strength through heretical collusions, but—in spite of mystical schools like the 'Thread of the Word' (Ka-Gyü-pa) founded by Atīśa's pupil MAR-PA and made illustrious by the poet Milarāpa—had lost sight of the true Buddhist light. Of the sparse ethics of Śākyamuni, of the Four Truths of the Enlightened one, there only remained a Buddha of statues, worshipped by mortals and upheld by deities and demons.

It took the intervention, in the fifteenth century, of an energetic monk known as TSONG-KHA PA from his birthplace Tsong-Kha ('Land of the Onion', today part of China) for order to be imposed on an alarming proliferation. Rightly named the

The white Tārā, one of the two feminine incarnations of the odhisattva Avalokiteśvara the Compassionate, represented with an eye in her forehead and another in her palm. She holds the Buddhist lotus. (Gilt bronze, Tibet.)

'Reformer', he attacked the RED HATS or Nying-ma-pa, disciples of Padma-Sambhava, drove out the wives of married monks, smashed the instruments of sorcery, and closed monasteries. To put an end to all sects, he declared them heretical and instituted a rival to them: 'Those of the Virtuous Order' (Ge-luk pa), nicknamed the YELLOW HATS. He established the temporal hierarchy of novices (t'ra-pa), the more learned (or exalted: la-ma), superiors (ge-long) and abbots (khan-po). He laid down methods of teaching and examination, and prescribed the conditions of admission and expulsion.

Finally, he gave his order two luminaries, temporal and spiritual: in the Dalai Lama of Lhasa and later, the Paṇ-Chen Erdeni Rin-po-che, of Ṭashilhümpo. As much a statesman as a monk, Tsong-kha pa prepared the way for the theocratic

kingship that was to continue until the ascendancy of the Chinese People's Republic over Tibet.

The Buddhas: Tibetan Yogo-tantric Buddhism imagined a superhuman universe in seven stages, reigned over by the Unique, the Primordial, ĀDIBUDDHA, who has created himself through his own thought: the naked blue-bodied ascetic plunged in an infinite meditation that does not seem in any way to preclude his union with his śakti, as naked as himself but white. Here the Abstract is complemented by what is most bound to the physical. The śakti represents action bound to motive force, the manifest answering to creation. There we meet again in fact the Vedic conception of Purusha (active) united to Prakṛti (passive) to engender 'what is'.

On this question of the Supreme the schools disagreed: the Red Caps (Sa-kya-pa) see him in VAIROCANA, the immaculate buddha of meditation presiding over the Centre, and the Yellow Hats conceive of him as the spiritual double of Akshobhya, guardian of the east where the sun rises: his name VAJRA-DHARA, the Holder of the Thunderbolt.

The celestial Court is made up of heroic buddhas, the TATHĀGATAS, old enlightened ones who preceded Gautama Śākyamuni in his last descent to earth. The number is, according to the various sects, four, five, seven, nine, ten, twenty-four, thirty-two or thirty-four; all numbers expressing qualitative space. Before attaining ineffable Non-being, they have each spent seven sojourns in one of the paradises and undergone countless rebirths.

The Primordial reigns over five buddhas of meditation, the

The Tibetan monk Tsong-kha-pa has been aptly named the Reformer. By founding the Ge-luk-pa order, he purified Lamaistic Buddhism.

JINAS (Victorious ones) or 'DHYĀNI-BUDDHAS' whose existence we have already mentioned when speaking of Indian Mahāyāna. They deserve a close study, for they represent the very essence of the present-day Buddhism of Asia, even outside Tibet.

The Jinas, Regents of Space and Time, share the guardianship of the world in the sixth stage of Paradise. Invented or taken over in the earliest stages of Buddhism, there are five of them, like the five senses, the five virtues, the five colours, and the five cardinal points over which they preside. Five is a favourite number in India; the sacred number of the marriage between Heaven and Earth, the spiritual and the material, between what immutably 'is' and the whirlpool of rebirths which affects both the human and the non-human.

These five motionless contemplatives constitute the first link in an interminable chain uniting the One with the manifold, the changeless with perpetual evolution. They represent the five episodes of the life of the Buddha—four belonging to the Enlightenment and the fifth the sermon at Benares.

The monks imagined them as almost naked ascetics issuing from a three- or five-pointed flame, seated in the 'adamantine' position, the soles of their feet turned upwards. Besides long ears and the occipital protuberance, they have a woolly ūrṇa between the eyebrows. Their hair is curled or worn on top in a bun and a halo fans out behind their head. Each controls one human sense. Sitting on a mount (goose, horse, etc.), passively receiving a monosyllabic invocation proper to him (oṃ, hūṃ, hrīḥ, etc.), allotted a colour, sketching a significant gesture (mudrā), he appears to us lost in the contemplation of universes at once unified and various, logical and inconceivable, moving yet motionless like a crystal.

AKSHOBHYA, the 'Unshakable', blue all over and seated on an elephant, thunderbolt or lotus in hand, guards the east. He is the old Buddha, vanquisher of Māra. He was worshipped particularly in China, under the Han.

The red AMITĀBHA, 'Infinite Light', watches over the west where the sun sets. He is a transposition of an ancient Persian solar divinity. He represents the Buddha plunged in meditation

The five Jinas or meditation-buddhas.
Centre, Vairocana.
Bottom right, Amitābha.

and evokes the limitless brightness that spread over the universe at the Enlightenment.

The green AMOGHA-SIDDHI, 'Infallible Success', with hand raised, protects the north. He is the Buddha who, sheltered by Mucilinda, king of the many-headed Nāgas, enjoys a bliss that nothing can impair.

RATNA-SAMBHAVA, 'Jewel-born', golden all over, guards the south. He recalls the Buddha of precious stones, born as a gem within another flawless gem. His gesture is one of giving.

At the zenith, finally, reigns VAIROCANA, of dazzling whiteness. He is the preaching, radiant Buddha, and he heralds Maitreya. He is the Transcendent, who, by the Word, makes known to the world the revelation no one has witnessed.

Loftier conceptions are superimposed on these representations. It will be recalled that the material Body (or 'artificial body') of the Buddha was made of four elements (earth, water, fire, breath) together with a 'Spiritual Body' with which the Perfect one visited the heavens, and a 'Doctrine Body' (or Collection of Teachings, *Dharma-kāya*), his true essence. The four Jinas therefore also represent 'governors of matter', a kind of 'small change of the Buddha', while Vairocana corresponds to the Spiritual Body; the symbolic wheel and the position of his hand (mudrā), whose five fingers grip the thunderbolt, translate the Mystical union of nature with the sixth element, Mind. Going up one rung farther, the Jinas translate the transcendental components: Dharma, the material essence, united with Buddha, the intellectual essence, produces the active power of creation, or Saṃgha.

But there is yet another Jina, the essence of Ādibuddha, who controls the other five: this is VAJRA-SATTVA, the Universal Soul, Wisdom, the Supreme Intelligence, situated above the central point, whose sense is Insight. He is always represented crowned and coming out of a lotus in the midst of a three-pronged flame, and he holds with his right hand the thunderbolt-diamond (VAJRA). It is he who inspired Nāgārjuna when that eminent doctor discovered in a cave the writings of Śākyamuni.

Vajrasattva, lord of the world in Buddhist Yogo-tantrism,
holds the vajra (thunderbolt-diamond), emblem of his power.
(Style of Kuttach, India, 8th–9th centuries.)

Each Dhyāni-buddha, passive and motionless, has a princely replica, frequently portrayed in an upright position, sumptuously clothed, crowned and adorned with thirteen jewels, sometimes coupled with his śakti in the position called *yab-yum*. AMITĀYUS, Buddha of eternal life, who holds out a cup of ambrosia, accompanies Amitābha in this way.

Nor is this all: each of the Jinas also possesses a creative spiritual reflection that is sometimes called his son or bodhisattva.

This archangel has delayed his entry into Nirvāṇa in order to combat the demons of earth and heaven, and to save mankind. Thus Amitābha has begotten Avalokiteśvara ('The lord who looks compassionately down') and Amoghasiddhi Viśva-pāṇi as spiritual sons.

These forces, with the grace of adolescence and a prince's bearing, do not, although active, leave their palace of crystal in the fifth stage of heaven: when they had emerged from the cycle of rebirths, the need to exteriorize them made itself felt, exactly as for the Jinas who, at last in Nirvāṇa, are no longer accessible and must be represented by a less transcendental son. The bodhisattvas are incarnated in a human being (as Avalokiteśvara in the Dalai Lama) or delegate their power to an 'earthly reflection' who will come to gain Enlightenment on earth and earn Nirvāṇa. Thus with the prince Siddhārtha Gautama: proceeding from Avalokiteśvara, he became the Buddha, the Enlightened, and he is portrayed wearing on his hair-knot the effigy of Amitābha from whom he is derived in the third degree. It is the same with the future Buddha Maitreya, 'The Friendly one', the Golden Messiah dressed in sky-blue whom the archangel Viśvapāṇi will send in about four thousand five hundred million years.

To give an idea of the complexity of the schisms, it may be mentioned that the Yellow Hats regard the bodhisattva Vajradhara (or Vajra-pāṇi)—the holder of the thunderbolt, the secret Lord, identified with the Vedic god Indra—as son of Akshobhya, and consider him at the same time as supreme Buddha and as begetter of Śākyamuni in place of Avalokiteśvara.

Feminine counterparts actively accompany the five buddhas of meditation: the three demonic buddhas who are only appeased by invocations, the seven medicine Tathāgatas of whom the chief is the blue VAIPŪRYA, the thirty-five confession buddhas who are called upon for the hearing of sins. A host of buddhas fills the universe: to the East alone they are estimated at five thousand million. But all these buddhas spread over the three million worlds and issued from a great primordial Buddha are united in the earthly reflection of a bodhisattva when he leaves the empyrean to carry out his work of salvation. Here we meet again the Vedic myth of Purusha dispersed and re-forming in Agni the Fire. To revert to the buddhas appearing on earth, they succeed one another in a fixed order and bear different names in different countries. They number between fifty-six and a thousand. The number thirty-five seems to have been favoured at one point, the first being DĪPAM-KARA, the Illuminator, sprung from Vairocana, who lived a hundred thousand years on earth. The most recent is Śākyamuni. Only seven earthly buddhas are recognized in practice, the eighth to be Maitreya. Certain sects consider that humanity is in a new cycle, and some reduce this number from eight to five, others to only four. It should be added that each human being is a buddha in embryo: in each is found an absolute quality (*Tathatā*) that he must rid of the impurities in which it is embedded.

All these buddhas have one common characteristic, that of the triple essence:

1. A mortal and ascetic body of creation (Mānushi Buddha), arrived at Practical Wisdom, for human activity;

2. A body of enjoyment, of absolute purity, in the state of Reflected Wisdom, for superhuman activity;

3. A body of the Law installed in the *Arūpa-dhātu* sphere in the state of Essential Wisdom, as the Supreme Being, the One.

In the fifth heaven we find, besides the bodhisattvas already cited and eight other archangels, the TĀRĀS, green and white, a double replica of Avalokiteśvara, turned into a goddess of mercy under the name of KUAN-YIN in China or KWANNON in Japan; MAÑJUŚRĪ the Sweet-voiced, the Buddhist Apollo, Prince of Controversy, incarnation of Wisdom, so wise even that he is the only one not to have a corresponding female energy; the terrible lion-headed MARĪCI, reminiscent of Ushas, the Vedic Aurora, who was wife of YAMA, king of the hells and god of death.

On the four lower paradisal planes—the realm of protective Desire—all is confusion. There emerge the YI-DAM (Tib.), Tantric tutelary divinities derived directly from India, and the

Ḍākinī (lamaistic Erinys).
Bronze gilt and ornamented with turquoises.
Tibet.

furies or DĀKINĪS who drive away the enemies of Buddhism. The Hindu Durgā, wife of Śiva, is found under the terrifying guise of the bloodthirsty goddess PÄL LHA-MO, who, in spite of her appearance, is 'The Good', always ready to assist the pure heart assailed by demons.

Lower down are the thirty-three Brahmanical gods (subject to the law of death and rebirth, under the supervision of the Yidams), the Prince-Lords commanding the armies fighting against those who scorn the Law, the eight implacable Mothers, the eternally cursed Titans, the Nāgas who engendered all the gods, the Yaksha spirits, helpful in spite of their green faces and menacing fangs, the fearsome Rākshasa spirits, the twelve Furies. And beneath, the host of the Invisible, protectors or enemies of the Faith, patrons or adversaries of men, benevolent, demonic, saints and cemetery ghouls, running into millions of millions.

All, from the Dhyāni Buddhas to the vilest ghost, are nothing but the sparklings of a single diamond, a partial glimpse of the Inconceivable; only Enlightenment allows one to perceive the unity that underlies all this diversity: a veiled impalpable entity, which is perhaps only Māyā, illusion. . . . And there we rediscover at last the true essence of Buddhism.

YOGO-TANTRIC BUDDHIST PRACTICES

Tibetan asceticism comprises four stages, each corresponding to one of the four Great Truths: life, mental effort, practice, and achievement.

The Tantras: We see the Mahāyāna Buddhism of the north orienting itself towards two types of practice, that of the magical tantras and that of the sūtras.

Tantrism, born in the far north of India, attained its apogee about the fifth century A.D. but was extant long before that: latent in Bengal and Assam before the coming of the Buddha, it had for a long time been practised by small circles of initiates and had given rise to an abundant literature, still scarcely explored today. It makes its appearance under the forms known as '*Right-hand*' (the School of Secrets) where importance is attached to the male principle, and '*Left-hand*' (Vajra-yāna), which relies on the feminine principle (*śakti*). In the latter it welcomed not only the benevolent or fearful divinities belonging to the native populations but also the male and female demons of the ancient Tibetan P'ön-po.

The believer who follows the rites of the Vajrayāna (Way of the Diamond, or of the Thunderbolt) finds his genuine 'Diamond Nature', the Vajra being regarded as the Dharma, Enlightenment; in other words, Ultimate Reality.

Although often bearing the same names, the Tantric divinities must not be confused with those of Bhakti, created by the myth-making imagination, invoked with fervour and love: they personify magic spiritual forces, steps leading the believer to salvation. Although they have come by an indirect path, they fit in with the Buddha's representation of the world as 'a phantasmagoria in which magically created beings are saved from a magically created suffering by a magically created saviour who shows the insubstantiality of existence'.

'The enjoyments of all beings and their possessions are conjured up by the Māyā of their deeds,' states the Sage in the Ratnakūṭa; 'this order of monks by the Māyā of the Dharma; I

143

myself by the Māyā of Wisdom, and everything in general by the Māyā of the complexity of conditions.'

It is not that the world, the dharma, and the Buddha do not exist: they are real, but utterly different from what we suppose them to be. Out of this grew the conviction that only the magical methods of the tantras could validly explore the universe. Buddhism then became a ritual religion, just like those of the past, offering power and magical protection; it allowed the individual either to have his most material desires granted, or to set out spiritually on the road leading to Knowledge. The mystic finds himself back on an equal footing with the contemplative realization of Nāgārjuna.

With a view to helping their neighbour to win his salvation, at least as much as in order to deliver the monks from the whole cycle of rebirth, certain Buddhist sects have made a speciality of the acquisition of magical powers. By concentration the monks claim to arrive at possession of the eight *siddhis*, the eight magical powers of a finished yogi: they will command the elements, put a stop to epidemics, subdue wild beasts, walk on the waters, remove rocks at a distance, prevent the putrefaction of carcasses, and even revive the dead. They will enlist demons

*At the festivals of T'sam, monks dressed as
demons mime the salvation, by a
bodhisattva, of a soul on its way to Hell.*

in the army of defenders of the Law and annihilate those who
attack the faith of the believer.

The Tibetan Mar-pa had learnt from his master Nā-ro-pa—
head of the Indian university of Nālandā, the Buddhist Oxford
—how to change his shape and size, to see and hear at a distance, to read others' thoughts, and both to remember his
former births and to read the future. He was able to migrate
from one body to another, leaving his own apparently dead
before returning to animate it—a feat which, for pure Nālandists,
scarcely differed from transmigration from one existence to
another.

This Buddhism, known as that of the WHEEL OF TIME (*Kāla-
cakra*), was introduced into Tibet by Atīśa around 1040, and
marks the beginning of Tibetan chronology, which is reckoned
in twelve-year cycles. It did not spread in the figurative 'realm
of Śambhala' but was within the reach of every believer capable
of following the arid hermetic law to discover it.

The Mahāmudrā technique: It will help here to give an
outline, disregarding the demonological practices of the Nying-
ma-pa 'Red Hats' which are Buddhist only in name, of the
methods recommended of controlling attention and imagination
so that they may work towards Knowledge. It is to the first
Tashi-lama (*c.* 1550) that we owe the TREATISE ON THE GREAT
SYMBOL (Mahā-mudrā): it sets forth at full length the technique
of breathing and mystical perception.

Physical proceedings are in fact necessary—although rejected
by the pure orthodoxy which holds that they detract from spirituality. For the Tantric Buddhists the body, far from being an
obstacle to contemplation, can even be brought to perfect health
thereby, and will take part in the effort of liberation. They base
their case on the experience of yogis over thousands of years:
the seated position, with legs crossed and soles of the feet
turned upwards. The 'cord of meditation' passes behind the
shoulders and, pulling the knees backwards, prevents the chest
from sagging. The tongue is curled backwards, its tip touching
the palate; the eyes stare at the tip of the nose. The heterodox

claim besides to be able to do without both lungs and to control the '679 smooth fibres' of the muscles.

Breathing has a great importance for conditioning the attention: a correct rhythm brings about a drowsiness of the conscious faculties, and creates a particular psychic state. The Breath (Prāṇa), whose control was long utilized in the ancient Haṭha Yoga, is breathed in, held, and breathed out, and plays a determining rôle in the free exercise of the imagination. The hermits claim that such breathing exercises create a fever that allows them to tolerate the lowest temperatures: it may in fact be the case that they obtain in this way a displacement of the metabolism. The Mahāyāna orthodox, however, have nothing but contempt for these long-haired hermits who stride naked about the snowbound plateaux of Tibet.

But the ritual act must unite the body with the efficacious word (mantra) and with the thought (trance or samādhi). The most accepted practice for reaching ecstasy is to separate the state of consciousness into indefinite thought and, at the same time, detached and vigilant attention, 'as your eyes see your companion and the road'. One must put a stop to what we might call the cinematograph of thought, and fix the attention first of all on very elementary shapes and colours. By the 'inward turned gaze' the adept is capable of 'comprehending' the least object, of identifying himself with it. Space and time are abolished, yet without falling into total unconsciousness.

The separation is not an instrument of knowledge but of action.

> If in this state one examines the clear vision of emptiness in all its purity it will be called standing still and movement combined, just as the fish swims about in the water without agitating the surface. . . . But whatever may appear in this emptiness, put no trust in it and let it vanish. Do not take for reality your own mind or others. (Aurobindo.)

A whole process in four stages must be followed to arrive at contemplation of the emptiness of the three phenomenal worlds —of desires (kāma-dhātu), of forms (rūpa-dhātu), and the immaterial (arūpa-dhātu). Yet at no moment may a volition

146

intervene. It is enough to use the physical as a point of departure—sight, hearing, respiration—and to let oneself go: only vocation and imagination are necessary to empty the mind.

1. The concentration of sight on a Buddhistic image or a maṇḍala, and of the ear on the sound OM brings with it the fixing of the 'mind's eye' on the principle of emptiness and prevents any conscious reaction to the world about one: the ego vanishes.

2. Meditation stripped of all discursive thought controls the imagination and prevents one from distinguishing phenomena: 'true' reality appears with the setting to rest of the mind.

3. The control of sensibility and the absence of desires and dislikes bring about an inner bearing consistent with emptiness, the very essence of things.

4. The breaking of all bonds with the phenomenal world, and the independence of all causes, bring about the desired end: confrontation with the three bodies of the Buddha, a pure vision of Knowledge (*Bodhi*) that nothing can any longer affect.

During this performance the monk sees his body undergoing a frightful decomposition—as far as to lay bare the skeleton—and then a glorious reconstitution ordinarily imagined as the breaking forth of myriads of buddhas from each pore of the skin. When all obstacles to perfect understanding have been dispersed in this way, the adept abandons gross representations still provided with forms

Lamaist monk in winter dress (Mongolia). (Citroën Mission).

and colour to enter a domain of well-being and peace within. These are only stages: one must arrive at a complete indifference for this ethereal bliss, and feel—rather than perceive—the universe. Few pass beyond this stage, which confers extraordinary magical powers. But those who, at the end of 'eight descents into oneself', have reached the formless ecstasy in which space, consciousness and time are unlimited, will have opened the door of Non-Being in their lifetime. If their heart, which is prepared for a life of purity, stops beating at that moment, the chain of rebirth is for them broken for ever.

> Deliverance is not otherwise obtained.
> Afterwards, there is no more transmigration;
> Be resolved to become Buddha.

The Maṇḍala: The novice or monk who wants to go further than the priestly routine, places himself under a master who teaches him by word, thought, or even simply 'influence'— sometimes at a distance. He identifies himself with this guide (*guru*) who in his turn had been identified with his, and so on back to the bodhisattva who set the train in motion. This form of Bhakti is called Ka-gyü-pa (*bka' rgyud pa*) in Tibetan: it corresponds to the human heart's yearning to turn, through an intermediary, towards a luminous Being that cannot be imagined or depicted but can be addressed, and adored.

It is only by degrees that the adept approaches the austere regions of limitless consciousness. He will be instructed, guided, often left to confront himself alone. Whether it is for the attainment of the active spiritual life of the non-active one, body and heart must be pure, and offered without reserve. Initiations, as we call them—in which there is neither mystery nor secret— range from the simple counsel of the disciple's spiritual communion with the master, to ordeals in which the monk tries to exercise his powers in a fusion with the Cosmos.

The teachings are not given without rites, and each rite is begun and ended with an invocation in which gestures are valueless, even forbidden. The various initiations have no virtue in themselves: practices and formulae simply create the inner attitude that allows one to progress.

One gesture must be performed often, if not daily: it is the drawing of the *mandala*.

Known in all parts since palaeolithic times, the mandalas (magic circles) are symbolic representations serving as means for contemplation. They are usually constructed by the symmetrical arrangement (in a square or like a compass) of forms and colours around a central spot, the whole being drawn in a protective circle or polygon, reminiscent of the eternal re-beginning of all things. Every mandala expresses the changing character, as well as the opposition and harmony of its contraries, of a psyche whose 'burning-point' (J. Jacobi) is found at the centre.

A mandala is always a material representation of the universe according to the Buddhist theory of cosmography. It would certainly require a volume to deal with them individually. Suffice it to say that the drawing consists of reproducing by means of sand, flowers, coloured pebbles, grains of rice, spots of flour, or cakes, the harmonious relationship of the worlds. In the perfect circle of a microcosm in which nothing must be forgotten, not even man, the monk builds worlds, planets, satellites, oceans, mountain ranges, and continents, not following geographical or astronomical co-ordinates, but mythically.

Hidden in the mandalas—of which the Tibetan kind are the richest, and, aesthetically, the finest—lies a primordial magic force. The setting up of a mandala in a state of meditation allows a man to reunite what is separated in him. He draws gradually nearer to its psychological components, and thus attains to knowledge of the Self. This process does not depend on consciousness, but is 'undergone'. The unconscious understands the language of the mandala, whose symbolic expression well translates the uniqueness of the present conscious of the primordial past.

The adept 'free from duality' (*nir-dvandva*) follows exactly what C. G. Jung has since called a *process of individuation*. He lets himself be guided by an active imagination—which has

nothing in common with fantasy or inspiration—that might be defined as the faculty of forming images. The symbols of the maṇḍala, according to the way they are drawn, quicken the primal psychic subsoil in order to integrate it with the Conscious. Their salutary action is only grasped by the adept in the experience he undergoes at the time of the drawing, without his intellect having any other function than to register it.

After a very long training—for the structure is extremely complicated—the 'lama' succeeds in establishing the maṇḍala in a state of meditation. Literally split in two, he then 'sees' changing and eternal forces operating. His aim is to cross all the barriers that separate him from the mysterious centre where the bodhisattva he identifies himself with resides.

O Jinas, deliver us from the world of illusion.
I offer you salutations, oblations,
confessions of our sins against the Religion.
I proclaim our repentance.
May what Virtue we have gathered be of advantage to us.
OṂ MAṆI-PADME, HŪM!

CHINESE BUDDHISM

Buddhism only seems to have penetrated to China in the first century before Christ, probably thanks to the collision between the Han empire and the Indo-Scythian empire of Kāṇishka. The ambassadors sent to India by Ming-Ti did in fact bring back forty-two volumes of Mahāyāna sūtras. Yet although traders and Buddhist monks came to the Celestial Empire and, even, devotional books and the little catechisms then in use were put at the disposal of the literati, no notable stirring of interest is remarked before the first century A.D.

The masses in China were in fact essentially animistic, and the élite deeply impregnated with Confucianism. As Taoism answered the human craving for magic, the special genius of China—non-religious, sceptical, good-natured, with a realism that accords great importance to the facts of existence—was little inclined to dialectics or to new speculations about the extra-sensory world.

Kuanyin, Chinese form of Avalokiteśvara.
(Percheron coll.)

In any case, Buddhism was too heavily stamped with Indian thought to be enthusiastically accepted. Deeply original, steeped in the antiquity of her civilization, China has never been one of those countries that submit to a civilization, but of those, on the contrary, that diffuse their own.

Everything, including the language—or rather the many languages—militated against the spreading of Buddhism. Few people knew how to read, fewer still were familiar with the tongues of India, so that the already very abundant scriptures had to be translated, in order to be learnt by ear, not read. The translation of Hīnayāna and Mahāyāna texts from Sanskrit, often into several Chinese versions, must long have presented an almost insuperable difficulty.

The penetration was therefore slow, fragmentary, and often interrupted. There was express opposition from the Sons of Heaven reigning in the third and fourth centuries: the Chinese were forbidden to become monks, 'this state being opposed to the increase of the population, and completely useless for industry and agriculture'. If an intellectual welcome was accorded then to new ideas by certain literati because of the interest they offered in their remoteness from the Chinese way of thinking, that cannot be called conversion.

The Buddhism offered to the Black-Headed People arrived, by the long detours that geographical routes imposed on it, with rather an Iranian, even Hellenistic tinge: we find the mark of these influences in art and design, notably in those belonging to the Wei dynasty (third and fourth centuries A.D.).

Between 150 and 170, a Parthian prince known to the Chinese as An Shih-kao introduced the cult of Amitābha, no doubt of Zoroastrian origin: the Dhyāni-buddha of the west recalls a solar god whose red colour suggests the setting sun, at the hour that invites contemplative meditation. This cult was to receive popular approval under the Five Dynasties and the Sung. With the early T'ang, favour went rather to Maitreya, and then later to Avalokiteśvara under his Chinese form of Kuan-yin.

The first Indian preachers to create a few Buddhist nuclei in China were the Sarvāstivādins, compilers of the Abhidharma. We have already indicated that this sect denied the Brahmanist ātman and only recognized the reality of phenomena in their totality (*sarvam*). For them, there existed no possibility of consciousness without phenomena. The first documents in Chinese on this doctrine were only written down four centuries after the composition of the Abhidharma in Ṣanskrit.

In the fifth century, the school of the *Sautrāntikas* ('whose teachings end with the Sūtras') represented Sinhalese Hīnayāna in southern China. At the same time, thanks to FA HSIEN, the Sanskrit Mahāyāna texts arrived by way of Burma and Szechwan, and were soon translated.

About A.D. 555, Paramārtha brought the AVATAMSAKA doctrine, known in Chinese under the name of HUA YEN TSUNG. Keeping the mean between Yogācāra and Tantrism, it is concerned with the similarity of all things and the interpenetration of all elements of the world. Thus no duality exists; the object does not differ from the subject, any more than Nirvāṇa is distinct from the world. Existence is in no way at variance with non-existence.

In 720 Vajra-bodhi, a pupil of Nāga-bhodi (himself a disciple of Nāgārjuna), introduced the yoga adopted by the Chinese under the name of *Yu-chia*.

Ch'an: The great evangelist however was an Indian monk from the Deccan, BODHI-DHARMA—always represented in Chinese paintings in meditation before a wall, to exclude the idea of the outside world. He founded the real mystical school of Chinese Buddhism, the Ch'an (=Dhyāna), a task carried on by another pandit, BODHI-ŚRĪ.

But the man who was to give shape to the Religion was a pure Chinese: HSÜAN TSANG. After going away to study in India, he came back filled with inspired faith. In 610 he founded the *Wei-shih* (Mind-Only) *School*, which was subsequently to split into two rules, northern and southern, the first rather austere and the other more adapted to the exigencies of everyday life.

The Wei-shih doctrine calls in the most subtle dialectics to give body to the Word, to complete the earthly Buddha and the glorious Buddha, Master of Saints, by adding a third term, and to attempt, lastly, to offer an image of the Absolute 'even beyond his revelation to the bodhisattvas' (Paul Mus). This was an extension of the Mahāyānist doctrine of Nāgārjuna (that of the *Trikāya*), an extension already heralded by Asaṅga: 'In the spotless plane, there is neither unity of the Buddhas nor plurality, for they have no body, just like space, and yet previously they had a body.'

The Chinese Hsüan Tsang relied on magical conceptions vouched for since the origin of Buddhism: the separation of the planes of reality, and the definition of beings by their being projected from one plane to another, followed by influence over these beings through the medium of the traces they have left on the planes from which they have vanished: this, according to Mus, is the magician's task. It is thus that Mahā-Vairocana (the bodhisattva of the Centre, regarded as the Absolute), having himself entered meditation (*samādhi*), can absorb all his Blessed equals scattered through the universe, since he has made them come forth from him in the form of mystical projections. This double transmutation is valid for all the great groups, each of which is equivalent to the enormous sum of buddhas, and only differs from the others by its ideal centre. As Hsüan Tsang says, 'They penetrate and overlap without meeting any obstacle.'

In this conception of a pyramidal system, or of the formless Absolute placed at the 'zero point of space and time', one descends again into regions where Bodhi succeeds in being almost material. Every man, however under-privileged, can hope to climb the steps that will lead him to the quintessence of limitlessness and indifferentiation where he will be freed— in a word, Nirvāṇa. Even if he is ignorant of it, he has at least the chance.

We touch there upon the very essence of Buddhism, not indeed as stated in so many words by the Buddha, but as Nāgārjuna brought it to us. It eludes not only our western understanding but even any intellect that relies solely on the letter of the scriptures. Its true comprehension belongs only to a more and more refined spiritual meditation.

Hsüan Tsang was not only a great mind, an organizer of genius and an eloquent preacher, but also a man of letters and a scholar. In his *Treatise on the Achievement of [the view that everything is] Idea Alone*, which has become a classic, he was able to summarize faithfully the esoteric meaning of the commentaries to VASUBANDHU's Thirty Stanzas, and, in particular, that of Dharmapāla, abbot of Nālanda. His disciple K'uei-chi wrote (*c.* 680) a a Mahāyāna encyclopedia.

Chinese Buddhism was finally to achieve traits of its own, attached to the Mahāyāna yet without being a replica of that found in northern India and Burma, and also without falling into the yogo-tantric deviation of Tibet and Mongolia.

It was in the eighth century, however, that Indian Tantrism arrived, via Tibet. It was right-handed Tantra or the *system of Amoghavajra*, preserved until modern times under the name of MI-TSUNG. This school combined two tantric systems each embodied in its own mandala: we meet with a 'Circle of the Womb' (Garbha-dhātu), passive and aiming at the spiritual, and an active 'Adamantine Circle' (Vajra-dhātu). The various elements incorporated in these mandalas stand for the multiple aspects of the supreme reality, MAHĀ-VAIROCANA.

In the ninth century Atīśa came to China too, and settled there for quite a long time to purge Mahāyāna of purely Chinese accretions which had already been introduced: Taoist rites, the cult of the dragon, divination, etc. *Yin* and *Yang* or the harmonious conjunction of opposites (heaven-earth, sun-moon, hot-cold, dry-wet, male-female, etc.) had been transposed in Buddhist practice into the juxtaposition of the twins VINATA, the eagle-goddess (reminiscent of the Vishnuite Garuda) or sun aspiring to what is damp, and her sister KADRU, considered as her spouse and always represented bent double towards the earth. Their union evokes the two wheels of the cosmic chariot which the Chinese denote by the name of 'Heaven-and-Earth'.

The disciples of Atīśa caused the three great monasteries of T'ai shan, O-mei shan, and Chi-tsu shan, famous for their pilgrimages, to be built on mountains. They imposed Sanskrit as the sacred language employed by the monks in their recitations of the sūtras, the public confession of sins and the reading aloud of the scriptures.

The detachment of the monks from temporal concerns and, in particular, matters of state disquieted the Court. Under an emperor of the T'ang dynasty the prohibition against being a monk—disregarded since 385—was applied anew. The year 845 marked the Great Persecution: more than two hundred thousand Buddhist monks were deported and employed as forced labour on public works, and forty thousand shrines and nearly five thousand monasteries were pulled down.

Despite the zeal of the preachers and the visits of the highest Indian and Tibetan leaders, China cannot be said to have undergone a conversion to Buddhism. Certainly there is no lack of pagodas where Kuan Yin was invoked, places of pilgrimage were frequented, some great monasteries were founded where mystics lived. Yet the Confucianism of the literati, the popularity of animism and an immutable tradition prevented the Doctrine

The Chinese Annamite bonze is a regular priest, mediating between the Buddha or the divinified bodhisattvas, and the faithful. He no longer wears the humble yellow robe, but a tunicle in which Chinese influence is revealed. (Huong tich, Tonking.)

Chinese head of Buddha.
Painted terra-cotta (7th century).

from spreading. A realist, the Chinese only interested himself in giving a historical character to the buddhas of meditation and the bodhisattvas. Mañjuśrī was a Chinese prince renowned for his wisdom; or the White Tārā is the princess Weng chen, second wife of the Tibetan king Song-tsen Gam-po. The Buddha, where he did not cede to the local gods, was recognized as their sovereign because of his earthly existence in the body of prince Siddhārtha, of the royal family of the Śākyas.

The bonzes mingled with the secular. Healers, soothsayers, intercessors with the mighty, go-betweens in disputes, they took on besides a capital importance in everything connected with death. They came to exercise to some extent a monopoly in the orientation of the soul at the moment when it is about to leave the body, in its pacification, before it sets out on the path of transmigrations.

The gigantic Daibutsu of Kamakura
testifies to the fervour felt towards Amida in Japan. (Bronze, 18th century).

Annamite Buddhism: Annamite Buddhism, very fervent in certain places of pilgrimage, belongs to the Mahāyānist cult but has hardly any following in practice but by the bhikshus. The populace combines it with more or less degraded Confucian and Taoist animist practices as well as with an active trade in fortune-telling. Buddhism, as in Thai country, in Laos, has taken to itself the reverence given to indigenous Powers. Thus to the worship of the Buddha, Kuan Yin (Avalokiteśvara) and Ānanda are added those of Ngoc Hoang (the Jade Emperor, Jupiter of Taoism), the gods of Literature and of Thunder, the Spirit of the Soil, the Kim kuang (military defenders of Chinese Buddhism) and various male or female saints honoured for their virtues or the undeserved misfortunes they underwent.

BUDDHISM IN JAPAN

It would be wiser to speak of 'Japanese Buddhisms' than of one Buddhist religion practised in Japan: more than sixty sects are enumerated. But the spirit of Buddhism, whose vitality is attested by 72,000 temples and monasteries, so far prevails that —apart from the Christian minorities—the Empire of the Rising Sun may be called Buddhist, inasmuch as Buddhism has been able to superimpose itself on Shintōism, the national solar cult (The Way of the Gods), while recovering the comprehensiveness, the purity, and the merciful charity that the Master taught.

Having rejected the negation and destruction of personality, incompatible with the Japanese spirit, Buddhism had become somewhat suburbanized and 'dignified' in the process of crossing the China Sea. With a desire for perfection and technical precision in meditation, it adapted itself to the spirit of imperialism, the enjoyment of life, attachment to the idea of an enduring personality, and a certain social smoothness that are characteristic of Japan. The cults of AMIDA (Amitābha) and of Kwannon (feminized Avalokiteśvara) satisfy an urge to find a peace full of softness for the soul.

No Japanese Buddhist sees a betrayal in the transformation of the Master's teachings into ritual cults. Rites, though they cannot free from ignorance, are symbols offered to men's weakness, clever ways of helping the mind prepare itself for experience of the Dharma, and to deliver itself from the conditioned world in order to attain the deathless plane of the Unconditioned.

In 712, during the Tempyō period, the Chinese Wei-shih doctrine passed over to Japan where it flourished under the name of HOSSŌ. Its chosen centre lay in a monastery on Mount Hiyei (Hiei-zan) near Kyōto. A century later the monk DENGYŌ, sent by the emperor Kammu, brought back from China a monistic doctrine which he presented under the name of *Tendai* (Chin. *T'ien-t'ai*). This doctrine rejected the idea that buddhahood is reserved for saints alone; it professed that the 'Buddha Nature' and Enlightenment are latent in every man.

But the Tendai soon gave birth to dissensions striving to outbid this broadening. Amongst others must be cited the *Shingon* sect (cf. the Chinese Mi-tsung) preached in 816 by KŌBŌ DAISHI. This monk had been in touch with the great pre-Buddhist Indian systems and professed a cosmic charity. 'Mahā-Vairocana, the Great Illuminator, is the all-creating soul. Everything that exists manifests his power. Even a grain of sand. Even a drop of water' (Anesaki).

Amidism: Certain of the faithful were not content with mystical Nirvāṇa: these conceived the *Pure Land* paradise where Amitābha (called AMIDA in Japan) reigns, and where the souls saved from rebirths are born in the mystic lotus. Amidism, a tenderly compassionate doctrine, answers the longing of simple hearts eager to meet an accessible consoler, who loves fragments of himself in all beings. Since Amida was not thought of as a total, vague divinity, the worshipper derived a sense of cheerful calm from communion with a personal god of this sort, imagined so close to humanity—a feeling particularly necessary during the civil wars that drenched the Fujiwara shogunate in blood.

In the latter half of the twelfth century, a dissenting Tendai monk, HONEN SHONIN, known as GENKU, founded the *jōdō-shū* (Pure Lands Sect), a replica of Hsüan Tsang's Wei-shih:

the aim is to be reborn in the Sukhāvatī (Pure-land), whence the crossing to Nirvāṇa is facilitated. A realist, Honen stated: 'The age is too far away from the Master, and has degenerated. Nobody can properly understand the depth of Buddhist wisdom any more. All that people are still capable of is an act of faith in the Buddha.' Since all beings form part of the mystic body of the Dhyāni Buddha, faith thus becomes all-powerful, regardless of moral conduct.

The Jōdō, which has remained one of the most important sects, raised Honen to the rank of its saints, and made a regular gospel of his collections of poems. Banished by the Tendai when he was seventy-four, the apostle in fact sang the solicitude of Amida in verses filled with warm charity.

> His light fills the world in all directions.
> His grace never abandons one who invokes him.

A branch of the Jōdō, the *jōdō Shin-shū* (True Land of Purity School) was founded in 1250 by SHINRAN, a monk of the Tendai sect. While meditating, he was advised by Kwannon to break his monastic vows and marry a princess. Since then monks of this order have married and eaten meat. With a pure-minded life, trust in Amida suffices to obtain everlasting bliss.

We must also mention Nichiren, former adherent of the *Shin-gon*. A unitarian, and as much a politician as a monk in his opposition to the shogunate, the Mahāyāna worship and even that of Amida, he assumed the name of *Sun-lotus* (Nichi-ren), which is applied to his sect; in it, the believer must be absorbed into a Supreme Buddha, motionless within the universal Heaven. Nichiren was condemned to death and only owed his life to a miracle; lightning fell on the sabre just as the executioner raised it.

JIZŌ (Kshiti-garbha), revered in China, at Tun Huang, as the good judge of souls, is worshipped in modern Japan as patron of children, pregnant women, and travellers. He is the merry pilgrim who roams the mountains jangling metal rings hung on his long staff. Numerous other deities preside over all the acts

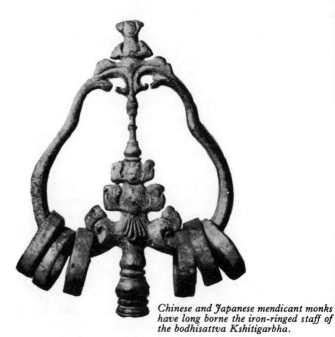

Chinese and Japanese mendicant monks have long borne the iron-ringed staff of the bodhisattva Kshitigarbha.

of common life, or embody traits of character (for instance, the Fox god); three thousand million *kamis* or guardian spirits of the Empire are cheerfully adopted by the Buddhist sects.

Zen: The dhyāna doctrine of Zen sprang directly from the Ch'an which the monk Bodhi-dharma had come to preach in China at the beginning of the sixth century. In an investigation of the 'I' the votaries of the sect tried to discover, through ecstasy, in the depths of their minds, the universal essence considered as the principle both of all existence and of all bodhiness. Much influenced by Taoism, Ch'an dhyāna considered forms only as the manifestation of the Invisible, a revelation of Ultimate Reality.

About 1190 the monk EISAI went to China, where he was an initiate in mental concentration. On his return he founded the ZEN sect at the monastery of Shōjukuji, at Hakata. Thirty years later, after studying in China, the monk DOGEN became the most ardent propagandist of the reformed Zen doctrine, to which he gave the name *sodo*.

Without making use of logical, 'reasoning' thought, the Zen follower develops his insight as a spiritual exercise: his object is to purify the soul of the troubles brought by habitual human preoccupations. Thus he discovers in himself the entity that outweighs and replaces all individual differentiations and episodic transformations—an entity that may be called mind, soul, or fundamental nature of the universe, and that implies the supreme unity always latent in existence.

The Zen discipline is practised according to the physical and psychic methods of Indian yoga pushed to the limits of technical precision. It aims at rendering the adept conscious of the primal nature of his Self when meditation has led him to identify himself with the Cosmos. There results an integral communion with Nature. In this sense this doctrine returns under a mystical and rather puritanic form to the pantheism of the Shintō cult.

The concentration, however—and this distinguishes Zen from Ch'an—aims at the development of energy for its own sake. A doctrine of disinterested and boundless action, the peculiarly Japanese code of 'supreme uselessness', it reached its greatest intensity among the samurai. It is a paradoxical thought indeed that the Buddha's doctrine of non-violence has ended in the warrior's Code of Honour (Bushidō).

It is a paradox, too, that the Zen exaltation of pure action should be so closely allied with sensibility—another Japanese characteristic. The greatest poets, the most famous painters, have been Zen adepts. They knew how to render in their verse or in their brush-stroke the intangible that lies behind reality, 'that subtle immensity in whose contemplation the sage finds his felicity' (Petrucci).

THE FURTHER SPREAD OF
BUDDHISM

It cannot be denied that the attraction of the Asiatic civilizations is increasing: a new universal humanism is being established that cannot exist without Asia's contribution. In particular, the study of the Indian civilizations, the Indian way of relating the individual to the cosmos, and their intuitive ways of perceiving, feeling, and 'speaking symbolically', have opened to us hitherto unsuspected vistas. However, the message of India is not that of Buddhism.

A question has therefore arisen—and will continue to do so: *Is Buddhism capable of being transplanted in the West?*

Certainly in Europe and the United States there have long been scholarly circles capable of an interest in it. Its diffusion was quite wide in England, partly through the Anglo-Saxon tendency to found societies and religious sects, partly through an undeniable popular taste—due to Protestantism—for spiritual speculation, and chiefly through direct contact with India. It is to the scholars of Great Britain that the greater part of the translations of Sanskrit and Pāli books is due, and in this matter their contribution to our civilization has been of the first order. It was in London, moreover, that the first European Buddhist Congress was held. In France, too, the greatest names of the intellectual élite are linked with a knowledge of Buddhism.

European men of letters in the first half of the nineteenth century who interested themselves in Buddhism include the Hungarian Csoma de Kőrös, the British diplomat Brian Hodgson, and France's Eugène Burnouf and P. E. Foucaux; such studies have since increased enormously, and amongst the many great names are those of V. Fausböll, Hermann Oldenberg, T. W. Rhys Davids, S. Beal, Sylvain Lévi, L. de la Vallée Poussin and many others. In 1929 a society of 'Les Amis du Bouddhisme' was founded in Paris on the initiative

The Sixth Council, held at Rangoon (Burma) in 1954, assembled representatives of all the Hinayānist (Theravādin) communities.

of Miss Constance Lounsbery, with *La Pensée Bouddhique* as its journal.

If, then, the West can nowadays refer to painstaking translations and very close studies for a knowledge of the finest dialectic, the problem arises of a penetration other than intellectual.

The Westerner's attitude may appear in three different ways:

1. An intellectual, humanistic attitude, illustrated in France by the school of Sylvain Lévi, in which Buddhism represents an important element of civilization.

2. An attitude that investigates Buddhism for the spiritual wealth it offers, and that regards its questions as real and relevant to us. Such is the approach of, say, Conze, who writes: 'Although one may originally be attracted by its remoteness, one can appreciate the real value of Buddhism only when one judges it by the result it produces in one's own life from day to day.'

3. A quasi-Buddhistic attitude (one that Count Hermann Keyserling caustically called 'questionable') amounting to a conversion. Its practical effect takes the form of adherence to a neo-Buddhism whose artificial character must be duly acknowledged and which, in Bacot's judgement, 'plays amongst living religions the part of Esperanto amidst the natural languages'.

Christianity has adopted two extreme positions with regard to Buddhism.

In the first place there is one of absolute denial: the Christian missionary Jäschke wrote angrily (in his Tibetan-English dictionary), '. . . Buddhist philosophy makes but a mockery of truth, by identifying it with a negation of reality'. More recently, R. Guénon calls Buddhism 'an anomaly, a profound deviation, a doctrine at once anti-traditional, anti-social and anti-metaphysical'.

It is undeniable that the negation of the soul as a lasting entity, the rejection of an accessible God, and the very idea of karmic transmigration could not but horrify a convinced Christian.

On the other hand, there are religious thinkers better disposed towards Buddhism. Such is Fr. de Lubac who, without departing in the least from Christian thought, does not hesitate to show the coincidences between the Christian's attitude and that of the Buddhist humanist; or René Grousset: 'The Christian can admire without reservation the many human beauties that Buddhism brings to light. . . . Without perhaps looking for Truth there, he will not forbid himself to draw lessons from it.'

When we come to the highest spheres of spirituality, the monastic ideals, ecstasies, and mysticisms of Buddhism and Christianity are not unlike one another, if they do not in fact coincide. Only the paths followed, the mechanisms, the 'declared' aim appear to differ. But when a Vogüe remarks, 'To imaginations warped by long sufferings Christianity has offered asceticism, whereas Buddhism procures for them the joys of annihilation', he makes it clear, in the context, that this annihilation is not a 'cold, black' death, but the fusion with an Absolute that the Christian mystic may call God.

Modern science, in its physico-chemical branch, has recently supported Buddhism.

The very latest conceptions of the atom have shown that, ultimately, it is reducible to energy which is transformed every fraction of a second. If mathematical laws are valid for a large number of atomic particles, they are not so for *one* atom. A synthesis is in fact by no means a sum of parts, nor an analysis a division. The principle of causality breaks down when brought to bear on the 'individual' atom, and only the uncertainty principle remains valid.

Not only has the image of the universe which our senses offer us been replaced by another image through knowledge of atomic physics, but also, on a philosophical plane, an insoluble dilemma arises from this new conception of the world. The energy data can only be established, in fact, by mathematical formulae, that is, by a mental process that speaks of nth dimensions which are inconceivable although they square with the equations. Now the human mind intervenes in these theoretical constructions; and so the problem arises of whether the mathematical physics conceived by this mind is true, and we find ourselves, as in Buddhism, faced with the impossibility of deeming our conception of an object valid if the subject is confused with it. Bertrand Russell has illustrated this by showing the incapacity of the brain to examine its own functioning.

This calling in question of knowledge is no less than the scientific recognition of Māyā, i.e. of the relativity of realities. To get beyond the barrier erected by the subject-object confusion, our only hope of escape is on a transcendental plane, detached from causality and the relation of the subject to the object studied. The farthest frontiers of a humanistic science thus end up in striking parallel to Buddhism.

An identical comparison may be made for another science: analytical psychology as William James foresaw it in his theory of discontinuous point-moments of consciousness, and as it is conceived today by the Zürich psychologist C. G. Jung. A perpetual state of flux between the personal conscious and unconscious and the archetypal collective unconscious; the coexistence of opposing tendencies; the interaction of all the known and unknown contents of the mind in its impressions, cognitions, and contradictions: in short, a series of psychological balances with no more determiniħg causation than that of the atoms.

And so we see physics joining Buddhism in its theory of universal flux, of the lack of substance inherent in matter, of impermanence, of fundamental error attaching to the testimony of the senses and consequently of doubt over the validity of the mind's speculations. We also see modern psychology concerned only with an essentially labile psyche: a fluid personality governed by temporary conjunctions escaping all control, and depending more or less on circumstances, acts, and thoughts either barely acknowledged or not acknowledged at all.

What else did the Buddha understand two thousand five hundred years ago but this?—that man has a certain vision of the universe through the medium of his senses; that he has another if he disengages himself from his sensory impressions; and yet another if he goes beyond perception of the laws that rule the balances of the universe and outside the causal sphere, to reach the domain of the unconditioned, which is as unthinkable for the intellect as is the identity of matter with magnetic fields and energic forces of attraction or repulsion. If we accept atomic physics as true, basing our view on the evidence of results, it is perfectly legitimate to accept the idea of vacuity, a state of unconditionedness outside phenomenal perceptions of time and space.

A change of perspective is beginning to appear, and science, undermining the world of appearances more each day, brings us nearer to truths divined and proclaimed by the Buddha. Foundations accepted till now are shaken, revealing new principles stationed beyond the limits of our understanding and yet perceptible by means of faculties whose use we have hitherto underestimated.

Must it be supposed that the moral, religious, and social truths with whose aid humanity has slowly emerged from barbarism are about to disappear for ever? One cannot live without some structural pattern; and materialism is certainly incapable of replacing those that appear to have had their day— for the very science upon which the materialists have hitherto relied shows us that what our senses can apprehend is tainted with the most fundamental error: that of putting our trust in tangible realities.

One is inevitably brought back to other conceptions of morality, religion, and human relations. And we cannot turn away from an Orient that, for millennia, has been aware of an indomitable spark that exists in man, a potentiality bound no doubt to a perishable body, but able to withdraw itself from a greedy attachment to the 'I'.

Going farther than the teaching of Śākyamuni, we must seek to understand the linking of destinies and transmigration as a heritage: the destruction of the walls that any human being tends to build round himself. The gods into whose hands we used to entrust ourselves have shown their powerlessness. But their disappearance has revealed a true God to us. Before him, man, emerging from the darkness of his affective, error-ridden judgements, will no doubt be able to 'grow'.

BUDDHIST ART

Buddhism offered mankind one of the most decisive chances to express its sensibility and spiritual aspirations in art. Yet it is notable that a flowering of Buddhist art did not come about until the second century A.D.

Perhaps the first Buddhists bowed to the wish, attributed to the Buddha, to condemn the worship of representational likenesses of his form. Had they qualms about giving precise shape to one who had preached the search for an extinction of form in order to obtain Nirvāṇa? Did the teaching appear enough to satisfy the spiritual needs of the faithful? As it was, until after Aśoka, he was evoked only symbolically, by 'his traces'. In those days, offerings were laid at the foot of a vacant royal throne, before an opened parasol with no one underneath it, before the Wheel of Life, a riderless horse, a footprint, the tree of Bodhi, and also on tumuli (stūpa, Tib. chörten): the latter sheltering relics commemorating some occurrence, or 'speaking symbolically' in a cosmological language.

The iconography of this earliest period was devoted only to the Sage's former lives or to episodes from his life as Siddhārtha Gautama—prior to the Enlightenment. In these first effigies we find an influence that, by the very fact of its being foreign, explains the break with the Indian tradition of non-representation: Gandhāra, a state in the north-west of India subject to Iranian, Parthian, Bactrian, and Hellenic domination, has given us in fact a Greco-Buddhist art of Hellenistic origin that portrayed the Sage with Western features.

In the following centuries sculptures, paintings, and frescoes were to create an atmosphere of faith and 'active charity' (Grousset). The abundance of statuettes and popular xylographic prints (votive offerings laid in the temple, pious souvenirs brought back from pilgrimages) was to contribute greatly to the spread of Buddhism under Aśoka and his successors.

The human effigy of the Buddha was henceforward adorned

'The Great Departure' of Prince Siddhārtha who was to become the Buddha has occasioned many interpretations. In this bas-relief of the Indian school of Amarāvati, the Perfect one is represented only by a parasol which a divinity is holding.

171

with divine attributes; he became a messenger of Heaven, and the bodhisattvas appeared as completely supernatural beings. Hīnayāna and Mahāyāna were moreover to make great use of iconography to develop in the individual the inner dispositions favourable to detachment: the contemplation of a Buddhist image would withdraw the adept from the outer world.

With the introduction of Tantrism the representation of the Sage, a bodhisattva, or even a symbolic object, became charged for the common people with an intrinsic power. Invested with sanctity, it offered protection and conferred invulnerability upon its possessor. As the teaching lost its sharp edge among the masses, magic gained ground. Faith was relegated to the background, but in the absence of Knowledge the lay Buddhist who addressed his devotions to a holy image acquired a sense of security.

All the Buddhist arts, sculpture, painting, religious objects, have been stamped with an ethnic and historical character. For instance, India at first offers us a certain naïve naturalism. Suppleness and a suggestion of the triple curvature (*tribhaṅga*) of the body mark the statues and bas-reliefs of the peninsula. The centuries brought, with the establishment of the Gupta dynasty, a perfection of plastic equilibrium, a religious respect that is not misrepresented by a refined elegance and a voluptuousness at once restrained and fervent. Form follows the evolution of the Doctrine.

The Indian genius paid no heed to the contradiction between the Buddhist attitude towards the body and the ancient Vedic sensuality. The Sage and the bodhisattvas wore moustaches and curly hair; their gestures were definite; numerous arms, emblems, and superimposed heads betokened their principal virtues. Whether the piece belongs to the school of Gandhāra, of Mathurā, or of Amarāvatī, whether it is fashioned in pink or grey stone, in white marble or in bronze, it always offers us a certain dynamic, distilled grace.

In Cambodia, after a period when the facial features were heavy and hardened and clothes stylized, Khmer art was inaugurated, all grace and all power, all delicacy and expression.

172

Supposed head of the Buddha.
Greco-Buddhist art of Gandhāra,
6th century.

The buddhas present a calm, somewhat square face, with clearly modelled lips raised in an elusive smile, lowered eyes, and an air of reflection and tender compassion. The head is surmounted by a tiered or conical head-dress with the image of Amitābha set into it.

In Laos on the other hand, under a Thai influence that prevailed over the Indian, the face is longer, rather angular and almost archaic. The mouth is slight, the lips describing two

*The serene calm of the Khmer portrayals
of the Buddha typify the style of Angkor (12th century).*

semi-circles springing from the root of the nose, which is long
and narrow. The cranial protuberance is crowned with a taper-
ing *mokhot*, whilst in Siam it bears a wavy flame.

In Java the post-Gupta Indian style grows heavy in the long
bas-reliefs of the temple of Borobuḍur. Although one can still
admire the graceful and restrained suppleness illustrating the
Jātakas and episodes from the life of Siddhārtha, the balance of
the compositions shows a certain thickness of modelling.

In China, whatever the period, Buddhist art always displays,
apart from a technical perfection in the handling of masses, a
stylized form that does not, however, prevent an extraordinary
dynamism. Naturally each dynasty has left its stamp on works

of art. Under the Northern (Toba) Wei (fifth century), the Greco-Buddhist style, which had undergone an Indian influence on the way, is elongated and made hieratic; the faces become mysterious, the folds of the clothing disguise the lines of the body—an austereness still in evidence in the Lung-men caves. Sui art gives all its ample fullness to forms that are still

Laotian art offers, in this Buddha seated in bhūmisparśa-mudrā, the classic type with the head topped by a flame. (Bronze, 14th century. Goloubew coll.)

a little static, whereas under the T'ang the pose becomes flowing and the drapery clings to the belly and thighs, making the divinities more human. Muscle assumes its full importance, expression is individual, and gesture is emphasized by a clever play of light and shade.

Sometimes the Chinese spirit, easily moved to raillery and derision, devotes itself entirely to the caricature of some small detail. It is also subject to the warlike atmosphere that has continually stained the Empire's marches with blood. The two guardians (the *Lokapālas*) and Mahā-Vairocana become muscular warriors of menacing aspect, brandishing formidable weapons.

In Tibet, finally, a strict canon imposed upon the artist has frozen art forms into conventional types that have not varied for centuries. Sculptures and paintings allied both to Bengali India and to Persia appear with a lavishness that corresponds exactly to yogo-tantric exuberance. Terror reigns supreme, yet without ever quite hiding merciful compassion. The gruesome is happily tempered by a Chinese contribution: in the tints and the delineation of small subsidiary scenes there is evidence of sensitive taste and a fresh naturalism that counterbalances the flames, the hideous forms of 'good goddesses', the death's heads, and the threatening gesticulations of demons enslaved to the Law, all direct expressions of the ancient Tibetan P'ön.

The canons of representation. There are keys that must be known in order to distinguish past or future 'dhyāni' buddhas, bodhisattvas and 'mānushi' buddhas. They are differentiated from one another by attitudes, position of the hands, postures, ornaments and emblems, animals and colours.

They have certain features in common, such as the *ūrṇa* or woolly tuft between the eyebrows, long ear-lobes, and the occipital protuberance (*ushṇisha*). The latter, in statues of the Sage, assumes the form of a tiara which is round (Gandhāra), conical (Cambodia), pointed (Siam, and Bengali paintings), or flame-shaped (Laotian or Siamese Thais). The hair is drawn up in a bun on the top of the skull or in little tight rings. All buddhas

Chinese Buddha seated in Padmāsana.

and bodhisattvas wear a more or less extensive halo, sometimes elliptical, and spring from a three- or five-branched flame. They are seated on a lotus whose colour varies for each of them.

Śākyamuni is represented in the lotus-position (*Padmāsana*), viz. with crossed legs, each foot resting upon the opposite thigh; in *Vīrāsana*, where the left foot is hidden under the right leg; in meditation (*Yogāsana*) where the attitude is similar but with the knees a little higher; in relaxation (*Sukhāsana* or *Lalitāsana*) with the foot hanging and the opposite knee raised; in royal abandon (*Mahārāja-lilāsana*) with the left knee lifted and the right leg folded on the seat, and the left arm resting on the knee whilst the right hand leans on the seat. Sometimes the Sage is upright, either standing still or walking, preaching or performing the classical gesture of 'giving'. The positions of the hands (*mudrās*) may be reduced to six:

1. MEDITATION: when the hands rest loosely on the knees. This is the *Dhyāna-* or *Yoga-mudrā*.

2. REASONING (*Vitarka-mudrā*): the right hand is raised palm

Kuanyin seated in reversed 'royal abandon'.
(China, T'ang era. Goloubew coll.)

outwards, the first and middle fingers joined or the first finger
touching the thumb. This is the gesture of Vajradhara the
indestructible, the Master of Secrets, the Supreme Being for
the Ge-luk-pa sect.

3. DAUNTLESSNESS (*Abhaya-mudrā*): the hand is held out,
fingers pointed up, palm outwards.

4. GIVING (*Varada-mudrā*):
the right hand hangs down,
palm outwards. This is the
mudrā of Kāśyapa, the third
mānushi buddha, who, buried
in Mount Kukkutapa, awaits
the coming of Maitreya.

5. PREACHING (*Dharmaca-
kra-mudrā*): the hands are
held together in front of the
breast to turn the wheel of
the Law; one has its palm
outwards, thumb and first
finger touching, the other
inwards with the thumb and
first finger touching those of
the previous hand.

6. ENLIGHTENMENT (*Bhū-
misparśa-mudrā*): the right
hand palm inwards, touches
the earth to summon it to
witness and make sure of its
possession.

These six mudrās are the
most common, but there exist
two others less widespread:

7. WORSHIP (*Añjali-mudrā*),
in which the hands are joined
palm to palm. It is principally
met with in upright positions.

8. THE MYSTERY OF THE
SIXTH ELEMENT: the five fingers of the right hand (the
five material elements) grip
the left index finger (the sixth
element, that of the Ādi-budd-
ha). This mudrā symbolises

The gesture of meditation.

The gesture of reasoning.

*The gesture of protection
(right hand) and of
benefaction (left hand).*

*The gesture of enlightenment.
(Finot coll.)*

The gesture of worship.

Mystery of the sixth element.

the mystic union of matter with the spiritual: it is the gesture of Vairocana, father of yoga, or of Vajra-sattva, the sixth dhyāni buddha.

Emblems differentiate the five Jinas: wheel, bell, thunderbolt diamond, lightning, flame. Likewise the five colours, whose union forms white, symbol of all purity. Likewise too the mounts: lion, elephant, horse, eagle, peacock. It is rather curious, in this matter of animals, to observe that the iconography of the Buddha Śākyamuni has borrowed from Brahmanism: for the Sage's seat, on which he received Enlightenment, has on it geese, the bird of Brahmā.

Finally a few words should be said about the lotus. This flower, stylized, drawn in a circle or not, and in principle thousand-petalled, is one of the characteristics of buddhahood. It figures on the sole of the feet and in the palm of buddhas and bodhisattvas. It serves as a seat: so that the Sage, regarded in the Mahāyāna as Father of worlds, is, like Brahmā, represented sitting in the heart of a lotus. In the centre is the secret four-petalled region where the creation of the universe was manifested: from there the secondary petals radiated in all directions.

It will be realized that the lotus is an aquatic flower that only opens in all its purity above the water where the plant has developed. Now the Buddha in Enlightenment is represented sitting in a lotus rising unpolluted from the earth: this miraculous sprouting stands for the setting free of the mind from the gross matter that the steps of the Sage had already levelled by treading it.

There would obviously still be much to say about Buddhist iconography: about Avalokiteśvara's eleven heads, the right-hand of which show displeasure and the left-hand joy; about the thousand arms of Kuan-yin or Kwannon; about the heads of Buddha where painting shows us three faces (the fourth being understood), standing for world-domination, omni-presence, and omni-activity; about the series of lotuses that grow out of an adept, each bearing a buddha from whom issues another lotus and so on to infinity. There again one might note a Hinduistic reminiscence of Brahmā springing from the cosmic navel of Vishnu, spread out over the Great Oceans.

I have only sought to give the broad lines of Buddhist art here, to point out its prodigious diversity and to mark at one and the same time the stages of the Doctrine and the racial trends of the peoples who have stamped it with their genius.

CHRONOLOGICAL TABLE

The peoples of India have displayed such an indifference for historical dating that it is always difficult to place an event with complete precision. Nothing was ever written down and the reconstruction of Indian annals has only been tentatively begun by means of the comparison of traditions and legendary accounts with archaeology, stone inscriptions and Greek history. Even travellers' accounts are of no great use to us: they are either too recent or filled with unchecked or distorted hearsay. The Indian not only did not deem it useful to write his history, but had no more respect in his legends for geographical extent than for the duration of time or unity of aspect. What does the exact date of the Buddha's birth or the actual royal authority of the Śākyas matter to him, compared with Immutable Truth? Even the names of great doctors of the Buddhist Law have remained unknown because of the anonymity that sainthood demands—and also from the minimal importance attached to a man's stay on earth, however great his learning or social rôle.

We are confronted, until the third century A.D. at least, with facts that have been embodied in legend without losing any of their authenticity. This statement, which pleases our Western intellect, is not in itself at all remarkable to a pure Buddhist. Above verified facts reigns a dominant idea that time has not managed to impair.

556 B.C. Birth of the Buddha.
> Peisistratos defeats the Megarians (565).
529 The Great Retirement.
> Death of Mahāvīra, the founder of Indian Jainism (529). Birth of Aeschylus (525).
519 The Sermon at Benares.
> Accession of Darius I in Persia (522).—Pythagoras. Death of Lao-Tze, founder of Chinese Taoism (520).
476 Death of the Buddha.
> Death of Confucius (479).—Birth of Socrates and Empedocles (470).
473 First Buddhist Council.
363 Second Council at Vaiśālī.
> The Ptolemies in Egypt (323).—Birth of Mencius (372).
325 Alexander in India.
> Death of Aristotle (322).
274 Beginning of Aśoka's reign.
> Italian unity (272).—Great Wall of China (250).
253 Mahendra brings Buddhism to Ceylon. Aśoka at Pāṭaliputra.
236 Death of Aśoka.—Mahāyāna is founded.
> Hamilcar leads his mercenaries into Spain (237).—The Hun empire extends from the Urals to Manchuria (221).
160 King Alexander reigns in the Punjab.—Original Prajñā-pāramitā.
> Revolt of Judas Maccabaeus against Antiochus IV of Syria (167). —Cato (150).—Siege of Carthage by the Romans (149).
80 Mahāyāna Sutra: Lotus of the Good Law.—Decline of Buddhism in India (about the beginning of our era).
> Sulla at Rome (82).—Caesar governor of Gaul, conquered up to the Rhine (58).—Antony weds Cleopatra (37).—Herod the Great restores the Kingdom of Judaea.

The Buddha was born with markings on the soles of his feet. Iconography seized upon this detail of predestination and multiplied symbols, notably the Wheel of Life, on the effigies it offered to the adoration of the faithful. (Angkor Vat, Khmer art of the 12th century.)

A.D. 25–60 Buddhism spreads in China.
   Death of Titus Livy and of Ovid (18).—*Beginning of Later Han Dynasty in China* (22).—*Death of Christ* (28).—*St. Peter and St. Paul martyred in Rome* (69).
78–103 ? Kanishka protects Buddhism in the north of the Indian Peninsula.
   Burning of Rome by Nero (64).—*Destruction of the temple of Jerusalem by Titus* (70).
160 Nāgārjuna.
   Marcus Aurelius (161–180).
220 Spread of Buddhism in Viet-Nam.
   Manicheism takes rise in Persia.—*Plotinus* (205–270).
372–390 Spread of Buddhism in Korea and China.
   The Huns in Russia (355).—*St. Martin of Tours* (372).
399–414 Fa Hsien's journey to India.
   Alaric besieges Rome and dies (408).—*Valentinian Emperor of the West* (415).
420–452 Foundation of Nālanda by Kumāra-gupta.—Persecution of Buddhism by the Toba Wei.—Spread of Hīnayāna Buddhism to Burma, Java, Sumatra.
   Death of St. Augustine (430).—*St. Patrick converts the Irish* (440).—*Defeat of Attila* (451).
498–561 Bodhidharma.—Great growth of Buddhism in China.—Oldest catalogue of the Chinese Tripiṭaka (518).—Spread of Buddhism to Japan.—Eclipse of Buddhism in Cambodia by Brahmanism (552).
   Emergence of France: Clovis (481).—*Unification of Japan* (520).—*Triumph of Belisarius at Rome* (547).—*St. Columba founds Iona* (563).
572 Shotoku Taishi patron of Buddhism in Japan.
   Birth of Mohammed (570).
573 Second persecution in China—in 610 Buddhism is the State Religion in Japan.
   Gregory I Pope: conversion of the English (597).
629 Hsüan-Tsang's journey to India.
   Mohammed flees Mecca (622).—*The Koran* (630).—*Heraclius saves Constantinople from the Persians* (622).
650 Amida Cult in Japan.—First Buddhist temple in Tibet.
   Saracens in Persia (651).—*Schism of Islam (Shi'ites and Sunnites).*
670–749 Gyōgi founds a Buddho-Shintōist syncretism in Japan.—Spread of Buddhism to Siam (720).
   Arab conquest of Spain (711).—*Charles Martel defeats Saracens at Tours* (732).
710–784 Nara period in Japan.—First monastery in Tibet (Padma-saṃbhava) (749).
   Pepin the Short crowned King of Franks by Boniface (751).—*Abassid Caliphate* (752).
767–822 Dengyō Daishi, founder of Tendai in Japan.—Mahāyāna prevails in Indonesia.—Buddhism supplants Śivaism in Kashmir.—Growth of Mahāyāna in Cambodia (800).
   End of the Lombard Kingdom'.—*Charlemagne crowned Emperor of the West in Rome* (800).—*Jayavarman VII King of the Khmers.*
837–842 Lang Dar-ma persecutes Buddhism in Tibet. Islam ousts Buddhism in Central Asia (*c.* 900).
   John Scotus Erigena (*fl.* 840).
1133–1212 Honen Shonin, reformer of Jōdo in Japan.
   Second Crusade (1147–1149).—*Nicholas Breakspeare Pope* (1154).
1197 Destruction of Nālanda University by Islam.
   Birth of Genghis Khan (1162 or -67).—*St. Thomas à Beckett.*

184

1202 Arrival of Sa-kya Paṇḍita in Tibet.
   Crusaders sack Constantinople (1204).—John, King of England,
      defeated at Bouvines (1214).
1227–1263 Tokiyori favours Zen in Japan.—Foundation of the Ikko sect.
   Death of St. Francis of Assisi (1226).—Aquinas (fl. 1268–1272).
1270–1294 Kubilai Khan favours Buddhism in China.—Nichiren founds the
   Hokke sect (1282).
   End of the Crusades (1270).—Dante (1265–1371).
1320 Decline of Mahāyāna in Cambodia.—Prevalence of Islam in Persia.
   The Popes at Avignon (1309–1377).—Meister Eckhart (d. 1327).
1340 Conversion of Laos.
   Enlistment for Hundred Years' War (1377).—William of Occam
      (condemned 1339).
1360 Buddhism the official religion of Siam.
   Black Prince (Poitiers, 1356).—Serbia and Bulgaria fall to Islam.
1392 Buddhism declines in Korea.
   Rival Popes (1378).—Wat Tyler (1381).—Ruysbroeck (d. 1381).
1400 Persecution in Annam.
   Timur reigns from India to Russia (1398).—Statute of Heresy
      (1401).
1407 Tsong-Kha-pa, reformer of Tibetan Buddhism, founds the Ge-luk-pa
   sect.
   Agincourt; John Hus burnt at the stake (1415).
1480 Hinduism replaces Buddhism in Java.—Islam replaces Buddhism in
   Sumatra.—Nobunaga destroys the monastery of the warrior
   monks at Hiei-zan.
   Inquisition at Seville (1477).—Birth of Luther (1483).—Savona-
      rola at Florence (1490).
1571–1577 Foundation of Kum-bum in Tibet.—Final conversion of the
   Mongols to Lamaism.
   Death of Calvin (1572).—Bartholomew's Day massacre of the
      Huguenots (1572).—The Jesuit Matteo Ricci arrives in China
      (1582).
1603 Tokugawa in Japan. Decline of Buddhism.
   The Dutch in Sumatra and Borneo (1598).—Charter of the East
      India Company (1600).
1642–1643 Fifth Dalai Lama becomes Priest-King of Tibet.—Construction
   of the Potala at Lhasa.
   Civil War breaks out in England (1642).—Jansen (d. 1638).—The
      Quakers.
1719 Mongol armies aid the Ge-luk-pa.
   South Sea Bubble.—Freemasonry Constitution of London (1717).
1769 Shintō becomes state religion of Japan.—Adherence of Nepal to Hinduism.
   Birth of Napoleon Bonaparte.—Vatican abolition of the Jesuit
      Order (1773).
1890 Revival of Buddhism in Japan.
   Cecil Rhodes.—Sino-Japanese War (1894).—Christian Science.—
      Salvation Army.
1909 Tai Hsü revives Chinese Buddhism.
   Union of South Africa (1910).—Chinese Republic (1911).

GLOSSARY

(Skt = Sanskrit; P = Pāli; Tib = Tibetan; Ch = Chinese; Jap = Japanese. Technical terms in Skt. where no other indication is given. It is customary to cite Skt. words in their 'stem' form, without case terminations, except in the case of a few words better known in the nominative.)

Abhi-dharma (P. *Abhi-dhamma*)—The Division of the canon of Buddhist scriptures devoted to the scholastic elaboration of the Doctrine (Dharma) contained in the Sūtra-Piṭaka.

Agni—In the Vedic religion, god of fire.

Ahiṃsā—Principle of harmlessness or non-violence. Respect for all life.

Ajaṇṭā—Village of southern India (Hyderabad): near thirty caves decorated with admirable Buddhist frescoes between A.D. 200 and 700.

Amitābha—Buddha of Meditation (Jina, 'Dhyāni') of infinite light. His cult was inaugurated by Saraha, master of Nāgārjuna, and has remained flourishing in China. His glorious representation is Amitāyus, Lord of limitless life.

Ānanda—Cousin and favourite disciple of the Buddha. He recited the Sūtras to the first Council.

An-ātman (P. *Anatta*)—The 'non-ego', non-self.

Āraṇyaka—(Skt) 'Forest Treatise', a class of Vedic commentary associated with the Brāhmaṇas and intended for hermits.

*Monks taking their meal before respectful
believers between the sessions of the Seventh Council.*

Arhat—(P. *Arahā*)—'Deserving', the (*Hīnayāna*) worthy man who breaks the 'ten fetters', follows the 'eightfold way' and arrives at the gates of Nirvāṇa.

Asaṅga—Founder of Yogācāra (450), inspired by Maitreya.

Aśoka—Emperor of all India (the South excepted) 263–232 B.C. He had Buddhist texts engraved on rocks, on pillars and in caves. He entered the Buddhist order *c.* 241.

Aśva-ghosha—One of the founders of the Mahāyāna. Great Buddhist poet (A.D. 80).

Atīśa—Monk from Bengal (979–1054) who went to restore Buddhism in Tibet.

Ātman (P. *Atta*)—Individual soul (breath), which is imprisoned in a body, and must return, after numerous metamorphoses, to the Supreme Soul (Param-ātman).

Avalokiteśvara—The most revered bodhisattva of the Mahāyāna. Spiritual son of Amitābha. The compassionate. Was incarnated in Śākyamuni. In feminine form: Kuan-yin (China), Kwannon (Japan).

Bhagavad-Gītā—'Song of the Lord', religious poem of devotion, included in the Indian epic of the Mahā-Bhārata.

Bhakti—(Skt.) personal devotion. Means of salvation, contrasted with the Way of Works and the Way of Knowledge.

Bodhgaya (Skt. Buddha-gayā)—Village in Bihar where the Enlightenment took place. Up to 1940 the fig-tree (*ficus religiosus*) under which Gautama sat in his supreme meditation was still to be seen there.

Bodhi-Dharma—Buddhist monk who came in 520 to Lo-yang (Ho-nan) to found Chinese Buddhism. Principal theoretician of the Meditation (Ch'an) school of Mahāyāna.

Brahmā (nom. sing. of *Brahmán*, masc.)—Personification of Bráhman (the absolute), as Lord of Created things (Prajā-pati). One of the three gods of the Hindu Triad.

Bráhman, neut. (nom. sing.: Brahmă)—The universal Supreme Spirit, object of abstract meditation.

Brāhmaṇa (neut.)—*lit.*, interpretation of the Brahman: the second division of the Vedic sacred texts.

'*Brahmin*'—Eng. rendering of Skt. *Brāhmaṇa* (masc.): 'one having to do with Brahman', a member of the priestly caste.

Buddha-Ghosa—Buddhist philosopher (fifth cent. B.C.), went to Ceylon to write the Path of Purity.

Bushi-dō (Jap.)—Way of the Knights. Moral code of the warrior according to Zen discipline.

Cakra-vartin—Universal King: the highest temporal power, as the Buddha is the highest spiritual power. If Gautama had not been enlightened he would have been a *cakravartin*. Possesses seven treasures: wheel, white elephant, horse, pearl, jewel of a wife, treasurer, and advisory minister (or seal box).

Councils—1st at Rājagṛha, 486 B.C., presided over by Kāśyapa. 2nd at Vaiśālī, 383 B.C. 3rd (Thera-vāda school) at Pāṭaliputra, 247, in the reign of Asoka: final secession of the Mahāyāna. 6th (Theravāda) at Rangoon, 1954.

Dalai Lama—Spiritual and temporal head of Tibet, incarnation of Avalokiteśvara. Resides at Lha-sa, the 'place of the gods'.

Dharma (P. Dhamma)—*a.* The Doctrine, the Law. *b.* An element or attribute.

Fo-t'o (Ch.)—The Buddha.

Hsüan tsang—(Sometimes spelt Yüan Chwang, etc.), 602–664. Chinese philosopher who brought back texts from India which he translated for the monastery of Tzŭ En.

Īśvara (Skt.)—'The Lord', in the yoga system.

'*Kanjur*' (for Tib. *bka'-'gyur*)—Tibetan translation of the Sanskrit canon in 100 volumes.

Kapila—(see Sāṃkhya).

Karman (nom. *Karma*)—Law of Causality according to which all actions, words or thoughts have a dynamic force that is expressed in following existences or wheels of time.

Kāśyapa—Disciple and contemporary of the Buddha, presided at the first council. Also the name of the buddha who preceded Śākyamuni.

Kshatriya—Warrior, noble, the second Indian caste.

Lama (Tib., spelt *bla-ma*)—'superior'. Title given to learned ecclesiastics.

Loka. 'World'. There are three—heaven, earth, hell—in the Buddhist division of the Universe.

Lokeśvara—'Lord of the world': Avalokiteśvara amongst the Khmers, and in the Himalayas.

Lotus of the Good Law—Sermons given by the Buddha on Vulture Peak near Gayā. Special scripture of the Nichiren sect in Japan.

Mādhyamika—'Middle doctrine' founded by Nāgārjuna and introduced into China by the Indian monk Kumāra-Jīva, about 380.

'*Mahatma*' (Skt. Mahātman)—'Great Soul'. Masters of Wisdom and Compassion who, like the bodhisattvas of the Mahāyāna, have temporarily renounced the completion of their spiritual evolution to remain on earth, immortal, in order to help others on the path of salvation. By extension, a term applied to great philosophers such as Gandhi.

Maitreya—The future Buddha who will come 5,656 million years after the death of Gautama. Chinese Mi-lo; Jap. Mi-roku.

Mana (Polynesian)—Anonymous, impersonal force, diffused in all beings, the basis of all activity.

Mañju-śrī—Bodhisattva of the Five Wisdoms. Ninth predecessor of the Buddha. He is the only one to have no śakti.

Māra—The tempter, the instincts, vitality. Reigns over the sixth heaven, that of sensual delights.

Māyā—(*lit.* 'illusion', 'jugglery') unfathomable force that dwells in the ultimate Brahman-ātman reality. It 'projects' the material universe and all it contains.

Nāgārjuna—(2nd cent. B.C.). Brahmin from Berar who wrested from the Nāgas writings put down at the Buddha's dictation. Founder of the School of the Medium Way (Mādhyamika).

Oṃ Maṇi-padme Hūṃ!—'O she of the jewelled lotus, Hūṃ.' Knowledge in the Mind, the Doctrine in the world. Buddhist ritual formula (*mantra*) whose recitation replaces good works. Tārā is invoked as Śakti (*q.v.*) of Avalokiteśvara.

Padma-Saṃbhava—Missionary from Kashmir; introduced in Tibet the

Tantric Buddhism whose esoteric and magical character was suited to the country.

Prajāpati—Master of Creatures. Personification of the creator of the Universe.

Prātimoksha (P. *Pāṭimokkha*)—'Words of release': collection of commandments whose periodical recitation is compulsory.

Purusha—The eternal, primordial man. The soul of the universe.

Śakti—Feminine principle which gives the deities their active energy. Of Hindu origin, it passed into Tantric Buddhism.

Sam-ā-dhi—Ecstatic consciousness, the last stage of mystical progress when the individuality is absorbed and lost, whilst realizing that it is one with the Unique Self.

Saṃsāra—Round of rebirths symbolized by the Wheel of Life. This embraces the six worlds of transmigration and the twelve stages of earthly life.

Sāñkhya (or *Sāṃkhya*)—Frankly atheistic orthodox system of Indian philosophy, ascribed to the mythical Kapila. Prakṛti, eternal primordial germ, comprises three essences: goodness, energy and darkness, generators of all that is and has ever been.

Shin-gon (Jap.)—The Sect of the True Word (=Ch. *Chen-yen*, the ordinary translation of *mantra* 'spell'), founded by Kōbō Daishi (774–835). The buddha Mahā-Vairocana is identified with Amaterasu, the Japanese sun-goddess.

Skandha (P. *Khandha*)—One of five physical and mental elements transferred from one birth to the next and constituting a temporary human identity. They are dispersed when the force that binds them together is finally extinguished in Nirvāṇa.

Stūpa—Raised monument intended to shelter relics or commemorate an event. Constructed in such a way as to symbolize the different parts of the world, it embodies the whole original doctrine.

Tantra—Tantrism, or any of its books. Originally composed for the Śivaite cult and adopted by Buddhism. They introduced the feminine principle as energy-complement of the deity.

Tārā—Double incarnation (white and green) of Avalokiteśvara in the two wives of the Tibetan king Song Tsän Gam-po, who introduced Buddhism into his kingdom.

Ṭashi-Lama—The Abbot of Ṭashi-lhümpo, honorary spiritual master of the Dalai Lama. Resides at Shiga-tse.

'*Wesak*' (Skt. *Vaiśākha*)—Name of a month (April–May). The Buddhist New Year, when the birth, enlightenment and Nirvāṇa of the Buddha are celebrated.

BIBLIOGRAPHY

Buddhist Texts Through the Ages (ed. E. J. D. Conze, D. Snellgrove, I. B. Horner and A. Waley) (Cassirer, Oxford, 1954).

Cambridge History of India (ed. E. J. Rapson and others), vol. i (Cambridge, 1922).

CARPENTER, J. ESTLIN, *Buddhism and Christianity* (London, 1923).

CONZE, EDWARD, *Buddhism: its Essence and Development*, 2nd ed. (Cassirer, Oxford, 1953).

COOMARASWAMY, A. K., *Living Thoughts of Gotama the Buddha* (London, 1948).

DASGUPTA, S. N., *A History of Indian Philosophy*, vol. i (Cambridge, 1922; since reprinted).

DAVIDS, T. W. RHYS. *See* RHYS DAVIDS, *below*.

ELIOT, SIR CHARLES NORTON, *Hinduism and Buddhism*, 3 vols. (London, 1921).

    Japanese Buddhism (London, 1934).

FARQUHAR, JOHN N., *An Outline of the Religious Literature of India* (Oxford, 1920).

KEITH, A. BERRIDALE, *Buddhist Philosophy in India and Ceylon* (Oxford, 1923).

KERN, JOHAN H. C., *Manual of Indian Buddhism* (Strasbourg, 1896).

KROM, N. J., *The Life of Buddha on the Stūpa of Borobaḍur.*

DE LUBAC, HENRI, *Aspects of Buddhism* (London and New York, 1953).

OLDENBERG, HERMANN, *Buddha*, 9th ed. (Berlin, 1921); Eng. tr. of 1st ed. (London, 1882).

PERCHERON, MAURICE, *Dieux et démons, lamas et sorciers de Mongolie* (Paris, 1954).

RHYS DAVIDS, T. W. (tr.), *Buddhist Birth Stories* (Routledge, London, 1925).
ROCKHILL, WM. W. (tr.), *The Life of the Buddha* (London, 1884).
SAURAT, DENIS, *A History of Religions* (London and Toronto, 1934).
SMITH, VINCENT A., *The Early History of India*, 3rd ed. (Oxford, 1914).
SNELLGROVE, DAVID, *Buddhist Himālaya* (Cassirer, Oxford, 1957).
THOMAS, E. J., *History of Buddhist Thought* (London, 1933).
The Life of Buddha, as Legend and History, revised ed. (London, 1949).
The Middle Way, organ of the Buddhist Society, London.

ILLUSTRATIONS

Guimet (Musée Guimet): pp. 59, 69, 142, 173, 179a.
Roger Roche (Musée Guimet): pp. 4, 18, 24, 29, 33, 65, 94, 119, 135, 137, 139, 162, 177, 179b, 179c, 180c.
Roger Roche (Coll. Percheron): p. 150.
Photothèque Musée de l'Homme: pp. 12 (Le Prat), 16 (E. Maillart), 17 (Kauffmann).
Collection Percheron: pp. 18, 37, 48, 86, 97, 100, 101, 107, 109, 128, 144, 147, 174, 178, 180a, 180b, 190
Réalités (Photos J. P. Charbonnier): pp. 2, 98.
Revue Français: p. 158.
Magnum: pp. 93, 186. *Magnum—Cartier-Bresson:* p. 164.
Tibor Mende: p. 88.
Archives Photographiques: pp. 14, 20, 22, 23, 28, 30, 38, 46, 77, 126, 132, 134, 156, 161, 170, 175.

THE SANSKRIT ALPHABET

The spelling used for Sanskrit and Pāli words in this book preserves all the phonetic distinctions marked by the Indian alphabets. However, the reader may well think it not of first importance to master the exact Hindu pronunciation of what are, after all, 'dead' languages: the following notes are intended only to save him from the grosser errors.

Vowels: may be rendered as in German. The macron ($\bar{a}$, etc.) indicates length; the diphthongs *ai* and *au* are always long, as are *o* and *e*, but it is not customary to mark this length in transliterating. *r* resembles the *re* in *pretty*, especially as pronounced in the U.S.A.

Consonants: c, j, and *ñ* (palatals) are like the *ch, g,* and *n* in *exchange*. Neither the dentals (*t, d, n*) nor the cerebrals (*ṭ, ḍ, ṇ*) quite resemble English 't, d, n', but the cerebrals are nearer. *ñ* is the *n* in *bank*. *ś* (palatal) and *ṣ* (cerebral) may both be pronounced like English *sh*, but *ś* is rather more like *ch* in German *ich*. *ṃ* nasalizes a preceding vowel (as in French) but assumes the colour of a succeeding consonant, thus *saṃgha = saṅgha, saṃ-jña = sañjña, saṃtati = santati*, etc. The letters *kh, gh, ch, jh, ṭh, ḍh, th, dh, ph, bh*, are like the simple consonants with a succeeding aspiration, as in *cook-house, plug-hole, hitch-hike*, etc.

Other systems: variant transliterations may be met with, and the commonest are here listed: ṛi (with or without the dot) for *r*; ṅ for *ñ*; ç for *ś*; ṣ for *sh*; ṁ for *ṃ*.

Mongolia and Manchuria are rich in admirably carved stūpas, recounting episodes from the life of Śākyamuni. This one from Mukden is the object of pilgrimages to the relics of an arhat.